The Dharma of the West

by

Jay Konik

About the Author

Jay Konik was baptized, raised, and confirmed in the Lutheran faith of his Austrian-born mother in metropolitan Chicago as the twentieth century drew to a close. His father, a Catholic from southern Poland, has always been very interested in pre-Christian European traditions and even named the author after the legendary leader of the Argonauts. After a period of questioning and soul-searching, Jay converted to Theravada Buddhism at the age of 29 and has practiced Dharma with a Thai community since 2012. He began following the path of Ásatrú a few years later and today practices a syncretic fusion of the two.

Jay received his master's degree in history from the University of Virginia in 2007. He spent six years working in e-learning in Silicon Valley and has taught at almost every educational level, from preschool to college. He currently teaches history and philosophy at a high school in San Francisco, California, where he resides.

Section 1

Basic Buddhism

Chapter 1: Symbols of Enlightenment

Trees are powerful symbols. They occupy a central place in the visual depictions of origin and truth in nearly every religion. Gilgamesh slew the Bull of Heaven while out cutting cedars. An apple from the Tree of Knowledge was so seductive that to obtain merely a taste of it, Eve and Adam defied the only commandment Yahweh had given them and brought suffering into the world. King David found his son Absalom dead hanging from one. Christ died on a handmade copy, and Christians commemorate his birth by bringing trees into their homes. Medieval stonemasons carved the columns of countless cathedrals to resemble trees. Ancient Northern Europeans saw the entire universe as Yggdrasil, the great divine tree upon which our world hangs from but a single branch, and worshiped their gods in forest groves.

All around the world, ascetics have gone to forests for millennia to escape civilization and ponder the mysteries of life that, among trees, are ubiquitous and easy to see to the observant eye. Prince Siddhartha attained Enlightenment and became the Buddha under a tree; devotees still venerate that tree's descendent at the Mahabodhi Temple in India. Visit the temples of Southeast Asia, from Bangkok to Chiang Mai and Luang Prabang, and one finds temple doors bedecked in resplendent depictions of the tree of life, with rubies and emeralds for leaves.

Even irreligious people adopt the symbology of trees into their conceptions of themselves when they think of their "family trees." The idea that one's ancestors represent their roots leads to the conclusion that they are the flowering of what those ancestors created and left for them. We create our offspring, wither, and die, becoming the fertile soil that enables later leaves and flowers to claim us as their roots. The metaphor is so obvious precisely because it contains a kernel of essential truth—that which came before us made us what we are, that which came after us carries on parts of what we were, but that which we are will fade away, and be no more. There is no escaping this fact.

In the face of this, what can a person do? How is one to live with that? These are the questions that each person has to answer for themself. The Buddha taught that coming to terms with and accepting the universal truth of impermanence in one's heart is the key to living without fear, anger, and other suffering. He also taught that understanding "clicks" differently with each person for different reasons; there is a difference between understanding with the mind and with the heart.[1] The Thai word เข้าใจ (pronounced roughly as KHAO-chai) translates as "to understand" but literally means "to enter the heart." I've always loved that Thais speak about understanding as beyond merely processing thoughts but rather as something accepted within one's deepest corners. Once one can accept human life's fleeting nature emotionally and not just intellectually, there is no longer need to be afraid.

My own experiences and contemplations along these lines persuaded me to begin practicing Dharma, or the teachings of the Buddha, in earnest and to become a Buddhist. Buddhism is not a religion that requires much "faith" in the Christian sense of the word. The Buddha instructed his listeners and students on how to apply the Dharma to their specific situations, often presented in the main Buddhist scriptures (called the Tripiṭaka) in the form of Socratic dialogues, and asked them to go apply the Dharma to issues as they arose. Those who became Buddhists usually experienced some kind of breakthrough in understanding, as I did. In other words, I became a Buddhist because practicing the Dharma *works*.

Therefore, the way to truly understand the Buddha's teaching, called Dharma, is by examining your own experiences and how they make you feel. For example, when I was a younger man, I wanted more than anything to be a professional musician. I couldn't shred like Hendrix or write like Dylan, but I wrote some interesting songs and played in some good bands. I really wanted to become an accomplished, respected artist. Yet as time went on, it became clear to me that the odds against this grew longer by the week and my pursuit of this goal was very taxing. It entailed a laundry list of tasks, both pleasant and unpleasant, but which included spending many of my Friday nights lugging heavy

---

[1] Some critics of Buddhism point out that in scriptures the Buddha often seems to contradict himself. However, this is a feature of Buddhism rather than a defect. The Buddha would use whatever analogies and stories that he thought would best penetrate the heart of his listener on the occasion in question. The details were far less important than the reaction they provoked in the listener.

equipment up and down narrow staircases in clubs, haggling with booking guys and managers, staying up for long nights, and so much more while working a nine-to-five, five days a week. The cost to my personal relationships was also apparent.

Music was becoming less a pleasurable activity and more of a chore that I assigned myself. In the end, I accepted that music was not to be my professional destiny. It was looking more and more impossible, and what I had to do to get there was becoming more and more unpleasant. This is to say nothing of what life may have been like had I achieved this goal! I remembered Kurt Cobain and his struggles with the consequences of fame and how the Beatles described the chaos of being in the center of Beatlemania in interviews.

My change was but a single moment, like the blink of an eye or the flash of a camera, in which the way I viewed and felt about the whole thing shifted. As I recognized the problems that my need to be a musician was causing, I weighed it out, and in an instant, I let it go. It wasn't worth it. After that moment, music became fun and pleasurable again because I no longer approach it with specific goals and expectations that I had created about respect, money, and accolades. I play when and how I want to now, and I enjoy it, but if I never touched an instrument again, I would not lament. That, I believe, is exactly how one should practice living, applying this lesson learned by the heart to the transient nature of one's own life.

Changing one's views in this way is a very powerful tool for creating internal peace. I've experienced this on other occasions as well. My last name means "small horse" in Polish. For years, this was a source of consternation for me. I grew up around Chicago, a city in which Polish was at that time more widely spoken than Spanish. When I would meet people, the Polish speakers among them would often chuckle when they heard my surname. This would irritate me, especially when an attractive young lady would snicker. Years later, when I was studying in Kraków, one of my teachers read my name from the class list on the first day of instruction and chuckled. "Here we go again," I thought, and when I reacted defensively, my teacher looked confused and said, "*Co? To bardzo sympatyczne nazwisko!*"[2]

I realized my name endeared me to her! I had always wished to have a more powerful surname, but at that moment it hit me that a cute name had its advantages, and that maybe those pretty Polish girls in Chicago weren't laughing *at* me. I accepted that things may actually be other than what I had accepted as truth before, and my desire for a different name simply receded on its own. I even started to like my silly surname.

This is Dharma as I understand it. The goal is to let go; the way to that involves seeing and understanding things as they really are and letting the comprehensive truth of a situation replace the limited picture one builds in the heart. That is the main reason I am writing this book. I think that Dharma is so simple and basic, and yet so hard to see, that it remains behind essentially all religion and philosophy. For that reason, I believe one can cultivate understanding by practicing any tradition. To make that point, this book highlights examples of this truth embedded in different Western religions. As a Western Buddhist, I've often found it difficult to connect on a heart level to some Buddhist concepts because the symbology and cultural references commonly used by my Thai teachers do not resonate with me, a being who has spent at least this entire lifetime in the West. Dharma practice is all about reaching the practitioner's heart on its own terms, and it is easiest to see truth in a way that speaks to one's own cultural and conditioned milieux. I will explain Buddhist Dharma using stories from the Judeo-Christian tradition as well as from a European tradition so thoroughly eradicated and replaced by Abrahamic ones that it is today relegated to the designation of "mythology"—Ásatrú, or if you prefer, Norse paganism.

The eminent historian Will Durant once wrote that according to the Buddha, "happiness is possible neither [on earth] as paganism thinks, nor hereafter, as many religions think. Only peace is possible, only the cool quietude of craving ended, only *Nirvana*."[3] In the West, religious attitudes are changing. Levels of church attendance are at historic lows in Europe and are moving in

---

[2] "What? It's a very cute name!"
[3] Will Durant, *Our Oriental Heritage* (New York: Fine Communications, 1997), 428.

that direction in America. It is clear that many Western people have grown tired of mainstream Christianity but still see value in its teachings on faith, hope, and charity. The irreligious embrace secularism (which Durant equates with paganism), and the "spirituals" look East. So, I think seeking Dharma in paganism is appropriate for our era. This is why I want to show why Dharma, universal truth, is to be found everywhere and that feeding the growth of one's leaves with what comes from their roots is entirely appropriate. Both the polytheistic and monotheistic Western traditions are paths to wisdom and understanding if one is ready to see the lessons in them. It is in this spirit that I hope you approach this book. It is my goal to show that the Dharma also lives in the West.

Chapter 2: What Is Dharma?

Simply put, *Dharma* means "truth." The Buddha described truth as coming in three varieties: personal, democratic, and universal. Another word for personal truth is *opinion*. Examples of personal truth include statements like: Chinese food is tasty; you look better in red than green; summer is the best season. The veracity of such truths depends entirely on the eye of the beholder, so to speak. Only the small matter of height changes the mightiest of mountain ranges to a mere pile of stones. Democratic truths are what Jean-Jacques Rousseau called the "general will"; that is, they are things that society as a whole has agreed are true even though some individuals may disagree. Examples include things like: taxes are necessary; police uphold the law; representative government is preferable to dictatorship; it is important to recycle and to not litter.

Universal truth, on the other hand, does not change under any circumstances. It is always true. An example of universal truth is that all things that are born will eventually die.[4] No creature can maintain its current weight forever. All created things will crumble and fall apart if not properly maintained, and even if maintained, will eventually decay beyond repair. This is because all constructed things do not exist inherently; they are made from other, smaller things, and the aggregate itself exists only in the mind.

Sariputta, the Buddha's chief disciple, illustrates this point while preaching the Sermon of the Elephant's Footprint. He taught "just as when a space is enclosed by timbers and creepers, grass, and clay, it comes to be termed just 'house,' so too, when a space is enclosed by bones and sinews, flesh and skin, it comes to be termed just 'material form.'"[5] A house is a pile of wood, stone, glass, and so on; the mind creates the notion of "house" out of its elements. When the mind accepts the existence of the "house," it may be dismayed when the sink clogs, the roof begins to leak, the

---

[4] The Buddha taught that birth is the cause of all death.

[5] In this case, "material form" is another way to say "the body." Bhikkhu Bodhi and Bhikkhu Nanamoli, trans., *The Middle Length Discourses of the Buddha: A Translation of the Majjhima Nikāya* (Boston: Wisdom Publications, 2005), 283.

paint peels away, or an earthquake flattens it. On the other hand, the heart can accept that the "house" is not what the eighteenth-century German philosopher Immanuel Kant called a *Ding an sich*, or "thing unto itself". Rather, it is a mental construction based upon a snapshot of a moment in the life of an intricate jigsaw puzzle comprised of parts, and elements of parts, that are each subject to change independently of all the others—and such changes can, and eventually will, in some way compromise the integrity of the "house" by causing some kind of "damage." If it can, one may not feel anger or frustration because their expectations are not being ruptured in any way. One accepts the "house" as a whole as merely a self-induced delusion for the sake of convenience.

Yet, our expectations play a large role in how we react to hardship. When we are injured, hurt, insulted, disrespected, disappointed, or otherwise upset, is it not the rupture of expectations that cuts deeper than physical pain, unkind words, "wasted" time, or humiliation themselves ever could? Who creates expectations? Forcing ourselves to admit that the fixed realities our minds have constructed for ourselves out of ever-changing elements and attitudes are wrong is the most difficult thing to do and what the Buddha asks us to try.

Take the notion of sexual fidelity. In our time, many couples practice some degree of polyamory, or an "open relationship." In such arrangements, it is acceptable under circumstances negotiated by the couple to engage in sexual relations outside of the relationship. The physical act performed by someone in such a relationship or by a "cheating" partner is precisely the same; whether it causes pain or not has entirely to do with expectations and nothing to do with the act itself. A faithful partner wronged is most hurt by the lie that the reality wasn't what they believed to be so.

And so it is with ourselves. As Sariputta says, what are our bodies but a collection of water, earth, air, and energy? Every day, each person drinks and expels liters of water. Can anyone call a single drop "theirs"? What is the body but a momentary and ever-changing collection and combination of specimens of the elements? Am I not physically different than I was yesterday? I am half a kilo lighter, my beard is a little longer, and my skin is a shade darker after a day under the sun on the edge of the Pacific Ocean. Should I expect my body to remain unchanged?

If one can coax the heart to accept that the "body" is a figment of one's imagination with no bearing in objective reality, bound to decay and cease functioning in one way or the other, one may fear death less. It is in this way that I coaxed my heart to admit that being a musician was not everything I had imagined it to be. In my mind, being a musician meant respect, the ability to be creative for a living, to travel, and to not have a boss. While pursuing that dream, I discovered that there were many less attractive sides to the job. By accepting that my vision of being a musician was a fantasy, and that the unpleasant side was tightly bound to the parts I liked, it became easy to let go of the need to pursue that dream. I created the dream for myself, and it was very stressful. Understanding this gave me freedom from that need. By no longer expecting fame and fortune to come from music, I became free to play for its own sake without expectation, or indeed not to play at all and write a book.

This is what the Buddha called impermanence, among the most important aspects of the Dharma, his teaching. Impermanence has two aspects. One is the physical change that affects every living and nonliving thing; nothing lasts forever. The other side is less tangible and is best illustrated with an example. I had convinced myself that the reality of being a musician would mean XYZ things that I wanted. I was willing to do the things I didn't like as much because I felt that they were the cost of admission. When I realized that one does not pay the cost but that the cost and the benefit are baked in together, I decided to put the thing aside altogether. The good and the bad are not separate issues; they are one and the same. If I want one, I must also accept the other.

The Buddha taught that if one values life, one must also accept death. Life and death are not separate things; they, too, are impermanent. If one can coax the heart to accept that one's self-image is based on the personal interpretation of an assemblage of tangible and intangible elements; that the physical underpinnings of existence are legion; that every single one of these is subject to change and decay according to its own nature and trajectory; that some change to one or more will at some unknown moment undermine the structural whole and cause its demise (or perhaps merely a spell in a sickbed); and that therefore the "whole" is merely a figment of the imagination, resembling more a single frame of film than an entire reel, then one may no longer fear death.

This is exactly the reason for the very existence of religion. Religions are naught but collections of stories meant to help people to accept and cope with their own mortality. Most extant Western religions teach that the soul survives after death and can earn some kind of eternal paradise through wholesome actions in life or perhaps faith in the mercy of Yahweh (which is the personal name of the Judeo-Christian god). They presuppose the correctness of the mind's perception of itself—that is, it is indeed Kant's *Ding an sich* that survives physical death. Hinduism teaches something similar. This creates hope that death is not the end and that a better world awaits on the other side, offering comfort to the believer pondering their mortality, the reason for the existence of suffering in the world, and other irreconcilables.

The Buddha, on the other hand, taught that the journey to peace need not nor should not look outward toward an externally created Heaven, the existence of which is impossible to empirically prove or disprove in any case. And even if such a place existed, could a universal Heaven truly be that? Heaven is also subject to impermanence and, in an earthly as well as spiritual sense, means different things to everyone. Would a bloodthirsty killer not find Hell more to their liking? Someone who spent their entire life associating the act of killing with pleasure may surely make their own way to Hell after death without compulsion.

Dante Alighieri says as much in *The Inferno*. The wrathful give in to impulses trained over the course of their lives to tear each other to shreds in Canto VIII, and murderers bathe in blood so keenly spilled in life in Canto XII. In Canto III, while standing on the banks of the River Acheron watching the damned claw over each other to more quickly board the boat that will ferry them across to the Gates of Hell, the narrator expresses his astonishment at the eagerness of those unfortunate souls to begin their eternal tortures. The Roman poet Virgil, Dante's guide through Hell and Purgatory, explains that the damned do not see their fates as torturous. Yahweh created Hell as an act of divine love in order to give wicked people exactly what they want.

> "Figliuol mio," disse 'l maestro cortese,
> "quelli che muoion ne l'ira di Dio
> tutti convegnon qui d'ogne paese:
> e pronti sono a trapassar lo rio,
> che' la divina giustizia li sprona,
> si' che la tema si volve in disio."

> ["My son," the courteous Master said to me,
> "all who die in the shadow of God's wrath
> converge to this (shore) from every clime and country.
> And all pass over eagerly, for here
> Divine Justice transforms and spurs them so
> their dread turns wish: they yearn for what they fear."][6]

Similar concepts exist in Buddhism. In a Buddhist *jataka* story, the bodhisattva[7] acts as a translator between King Assaka, distraught over his dead wife, Ubbari, and Ubbari herself, who had been reborn as a dung worm. She is so caught up in her life and her desires as a dung worm that she could not see beyond that context and aspire to regain human birth nor to rejoin her former husband. Her new perception of reality had conditioned her to accept as normal, or even desirable, things that as a human she would have found revolting.

The Buddha did not teach us to hope for something more desirable beyond the horizon in this world or the next. Hope for a certain outcome in an ever-changing and uncertain universe beyond the control of one individual, let alone humanity as a

---

[6] Dante Alighieri, *The Divine Comedy,* trans. John Ciardi (New York: New American Library, 2003), 34.

[7] A bodhisattva is a "Buddha to be." Ages ago, before he attained Enlightenment, the being who would one day become Gotama Buddha aspired to become a Buddha and spent countless lives perfecting his character and preparing to become one. During this time, he was a bodhisattva. After achieving Buddhahood, he told *jataka* stories of his previous births as a way to teach moral and metaphysical principles to his disciples.

whole, is an exercise in futility. Following this path may also lead us to hope and wish for horrifying things, blind to potential consequences or, as in the case of Dante's damned souls or of Queen Ubbari, the larger context of one's situation.

Instead, the Buddha urged us to look inward, teaching us that perfect peace is available to us right here in this life if we seek it. Peace is to be found not in working toward hopeful dreams of changing a world one cannot control but rather in a surrender to the truth that change will happen on its own, even to ourselves, and one cannot predict its results nor greatly influence its direction. The Buddha asked us to hold our views and assumptions about good and evil, mine and not-mine, life and death, up to what he called the Four Noble Truths. They are:

1. *Dukkhā*, or suffering. There is suffering in this world. All people know this intuitively as everyone has experienced it in some way.
2. *Annichā*, or impermanence. The cause of suffering is our inability to accept that many of our views and assumptions about ourselves are based on notions of permanence (e.g., "*Cogito ergo sum*") and do not reflect reality as it is. In other words, the world does not and cannot conform to our expectations, and yet we refuse to adjust said expectations.
3. *Nirodhā*, or cessation. There is a way to end suffering.
4. *Maggā*, or path. There are eight steps to end suffering, with the most important being the first, Right View. If one can coax the heart to accept reality as it is, one will have fewer needs and conditions for happiness (or ideally none at all) and will not be disturbed by sudden and unexpected change, nor have any difficulty discerning and carrying out proper action in line with universal truth, called Dharma.

Section 2

The Judeo-Christian Tradition

Chapter 3: The Tree of Knowledge

Nearly every culture has a creation myth, and nearly each of these seeks to answer two essential questions: how did the world come to be, and how did humans emerge upon it?

Answers to the first question vary from the Earth being made from the corpses of divine beings (as in Germanic and some Native American beliefs); being the result of a sudden explosion of light and life into darkness and chaos, as the Greeks believed; or being the result of divine love, as in Egyptian stories. Uniquely Abrahamic is belief in the immortality of the creator, the entire universe being like some kind of project he began one day and whose ultimate destruction he will survive.

The Book of Genesis is quite clear about the nature of duality: "In the beginning . . . the earth was without form, and void; and darkness was upon the face of the deep . . . and God said, Let there be light: and there was light. And God saw the light, that it was good: and God divided the light from the darkness. And God called the light Day, and the darkness he called Night."[8] One moment, nothing was, and in the next, there was something!

In other words, existence only comes into being at all with the introduction of duality. Nothing can exist in this world without its opposite. There can be no concept of 'up' unless something else is 'down.' There can be no 'beauty' without something else that is 'ugly,' nor can there be 'we' without 'they' (a concept that the political history of the last century and a half in particular has repeatedly and clearly demonstrated). There can be no life without death, nor the converse. Duality is the nature of all things (a concept the Buddha called impermanence).

As to the second question, modern science teaches that humans are nothing more than a species of animal for which intelligence became the primary trait favored by natural selection. We are, essentially, animals whose big brains are their primary survival tools, making us better than others at thinking, in the same way that a fish with bigger fins is better at swimming or a bird with lighter bones flies with less effort than its counterparts. There is nothing particularly divine or unique about the process of our

---

[8] Gen. 1:2–5 (AV).

intelligence's evolution; it is an adaptation like any other. What makes it special are the side effects of having the capacity for rational and abstract thought beyond its use for survival itself.

Yet, nearly every creation story assigns a special place in the hierarchy of creation to humanity, treating animals as a part of the wider world and setting humans apart as a wholly new thing. We are somehow special and *superior* to other animals *because of* our intelligence and capacity to better understand the world. Once we learned how to manipulate the world to our liking, the separation was unmendable. Consider as an example the Sumerian *Epic of Gilgamesh*, the oldest extant story. The civilized King Gilgamesh could not best Enkidu, raised in the wild by animals, in direct combat, so he sent a prostitute with a jug of wine to soften up his challenger. The plan worked; the scent of woman and wine that clung to his body caused Enkidu's animal companions to shun him. Enkidu had crossed the line from animal to human, severing his bond with nature and marking him out as different, special. In the Jewish Bible, Yahweh waited until the last day of creation to make humans, spending a whole day making just two creatures (and one was a copy-and-paste with a few alterations!) while making *all the oceans* on an earlier day, *all the land* the next, and *all the animals* on another.

The recognition and acceptance of duality is the threshold for the emergence of the human race in most creation narratives. For example, in Genesis, Adam and Eve were innocent before they tasted the fruit of the Tree of Knowledge; they knew nothing of suffering. Yet it is precisely the knowledge of suffering (and of duality), to know that the "day ye eat thereof, then your eyes shall be opened, and ye shall be as gods, knowing good and evil,"[9] that tempted them. The serpent promises Eve and Adam that they will understand the dualistic nature of the universe: good and evil, birth and death, happiness and suffering, naked and clothed. Genesis reads, "He did eat. And the eyes of them both were opened, and they knew that they were naked; and they sewed fig leaves together, and made themselves aprons."[10]

---

[9] Gen. 3:5 (AV).
[10] Gen. 3:6–7 (AV).

Before they ate from the Tree of Knowledge, Adam and Eve did not understand the difference between the concepts of 'naked' and 'clothed' any more than does a bear or a fish, nor that one should be more or less shameful than the other. When the perception of duality entered their minds, they judged one state to be good and the other to be bad. The creation of a bad state caused their minds to want to avoid that which, before their minds changed, would have not chagrined them. Nothing changed except their perceptions, and this created emotions of shame, fear, and frustration where before there were none. That is how Yahweh knew they had eaten from the tree! Yahweh admits that he is the source of duality, namely good and evil, in the Book of Isaiah: "I form the light, and create darkness: I make peace, and create evil: I the Lord do all these things."[11] Good and evil are two sides of the same thing, one cannot exist without the other, and Yahweh is the source of both. Calling out Adam and Eve is a case of "real recognize real," as the expression goes.

This story perfectly illustrates the Buddhist explanation of the emergence of suffering as caused by impermanence. Adam and Eve had human bodies. Only when they began to assign dualistic notions of good and bad to them did they begin to suffer. Before eating the fruit, nakedness did not shame Eve and Adam because they did not see a difference between the naked and clothed states. But upon recognizing this difference, they quickly made clothes to hide their bodies. Their minds identified one state as desirable and another as undesirable. The latter must be avoided at all costs to avoid the associated distress, and the former must be pursued at all costs, for it becomes the way to what the mind perceives as happiness. They created a need out of nothing. And yet, what caused this question to arise in their minds but their minds themselves? What stands in the way of the mind letting go but the mind itself?

It reminds me of my own struggle to become a professional musician. I had always loved music as a child; my father, though the furthest thing from a musician himself, exposed me to many kinds of music, from the Beatles to Black Sabbath to Beethoven. I always associated music with fun and freedom and

---

[11] Isaiah 45:7 (AV).

self-expression. Then, one day when I was a teenager, I noticed that many of my peers admired and respected rock musicians. My view of music began to change. Rather than seeing it for what it is—aesthetically pleasing sound—I, like Eve and Adam, "drank the Kool-Aid" (in the parlance of our times) and changed my view of music. It became something one could use to become successful and respected as a creative type! To me, anything less meant failing at music. As I've described above, this created a lot of stress and difficulty for me.

It wasn't until I let go of this view that success with music meant being a rockstar that I could stop suffering over it. Once I did that, it became fun and divertive for me again. As I wrote in the previous chapter, I did so by examining the impermanence of the situation. What I thought it could or should be was quite different from the reality I was living while attempting to make a living from music. I was asking the wrong questions. I began to see the other side (see chapter 1), and once I saw the entire picture, I was able to drop my dualistic notions. The good and the bad were all part of being an ambitious musician. If I wanted to lose the bad, I had to stop needing the good. Aesthetically pleasing sounds should not cause so much stress. They are just ethereal, ungraspable vibrations in the air. To wish for anything more from them than momentary enjoyment causes one to inflict a lot of potential pitfalls on oneself, as my own experiences taught me.

In other words, once I realized that I didn't have to be a rockstar to enjoy listening to and making music, that fame has its price, and that I could make a good living in other ways that I also enjoy, I didn't feel any more need to subject myself to difficulty than Adam and Eve felt the need to make clothing before they had eaten from the Tree of Knowledge. Had they seen that their shame came only from creating duality in themselves and tacking to one side, they could have saved themselves the trouble of weaving clothes on a belly full of fruit.

It is only when Adam and Eve eat the fruit that they truly become *human*, with the potential for knowledge of both physical *and* metaphysical truth. This separated them from the rest of the animals, as wine separated Enkidu from his wild origins, and is indeed what most people, from a religious and scientific perspective, believe defines the *homo sapiens,* or literally, "wise man." Humans are uniquely able to internalize, personalize, and anticipate suffering, and therefore to make moral choices. Based on these choices, we form societies and do things like compromise, build on older knowledge, and preserve our memories in the written word.

The Buddha taught much the same thing when he said that human birth is the most precious of all possible births (see chapter 7) because humans have the greatest potential for enlightenment. Births lower than the human include animals, demons, and denizens of various hells. Higher births encompass many layers of heavenly realms, with more power and pleasure accorded to those with better karma, or in other words, those who have earned them through good moral actions.[12] Beings born in the lower realms are too preoccupied with their own suffering to give much thought to its origin and resolution, and those above are too preoccupied with pleasure. The human birth is right in between extremes; there is balance between pleasure and suffering. Humans experience enough suffering to contemplate and recognize the truth of impermanence, enough joy to define what suffering is, and enough moments in the middle to contemplate the relationship between the two. In other words, we have enough experience with both to compare observable physical and internal metaphysical truths on an intuitive level.

The Biblical story of creation is of the emergence of duality. Yahweh created light and dark, sea and land, animal and man. The Bible states quite explicitly that suffering entered the world only when Adam and Eve recognized duality. This is exactly as the Buddha taught. Seeing things that are in truth one as dualistic is the cause of suffering. The only thing that changed when Eve and Adam ate from the Tree of Knowledge was within them; they saw the world differently. They understood good and evil. Nakedness became evil and clothing became good, and what previously caused them no trouble became a source of suffering.

---

[12] Interestingly, the idea of Heaven not being an equal experience for all, but one of hierarchical levels of ecstasy, also shows up in Christian writings. For example, in Dante's *Paradiso*, the blessed are sorted according to merit. Prophets, saints, and the like dwell far closer to the Empyrean than those who, for example, pursued the Good but for selfish reasons, or those inconstant in their vows.

Similarly, seeing life and death as separate, with one good and the other bad, causes everyone suffering. However, life and death are parts of the same thing. One cannot separate life and death just as one cannot separate the states of nakedness and being clothed. They define each other and interchange as part of physical existence. Impossibly clinging to one and avoiding the other is the state within us that causes fear, anger, and hatred. Recognizing that duality and separation exist only in the mind and that holding onto them causes one to suffer is the way to the end of suffering. The Jewish story of the Tree of Knowledge contains this immutable truth and displays it in beautiful metaphor. We are only human because we suffer, and we suffer only because of the concepts and beliefs we hold in our heart that contradict or bend universal, inescapable truth. So in that way I disagree with the writer of Genesis. I don't know if he made the world or not, nor if he molded clay into Adam's body, but Yahweh did not make man; man made man when he ate from the Tree of Knowledge.

Both Jesus Christ and the Buddha taught using parables, stories designed to teach a moral lesson. As I've mentioned earlier, the Buddha's parables could take many forms: sometimes he would invent a story, and other times he would tell a story of one of his previous births in which he corrected some wrong view of his or, in a *jataka* story, how he perhaps helped someone else do the same. Sometimes, he would relate a story from one of the listener's own previous lives. The Buddha would offer whatever story he felt the listener needed to hear to learn the lesson that the Buddha wanted to teach and would help them internally apply the lesson to their own life and context in order to internalize the teaching.

Similarly, one of Christ's more famous sayings is "He that is without sin among you, let him first cast a stone."[13] By saying this, he is not advocating stoning people, but rather underlining his point about combating one's inner attachments. Like the Buddha, Christ invites us to look inward and internalize. Rather than condemn a woman for committing adultery, it is better to go inward and ask yourself why you may have done something dishonest or hurtful in your own life.[14] The answer can lead you to discover your own permanent views that cause you to act in ways that, when others do so, seem abhorrent.

Christ illustrated these principles in parables. He told stories about people and situations he would invent, or perhaps things he had witnessed during the period of his life between adolescence and roughly age thirty, about which the Bible is strangely silent. Nevertheless, Christ's parables performed a function similar to that of the Buddha's lessons. Both would illustrate how holding wrong views based on something permanent would cause suffering. To that end, I think it would be profitable to discuss two of Christ's parables. The first comes from the twentieth chapter of Matthew (verses 1–16) and is often referred to as the parable of the laborers in the vineyard. The second comes from the sixteenth

---

[13] John 8:7 (AV).

[14] Incidentally, Confucius urges the same, writing in Book Four of *The Analects*: "When you come across a superior person, think of being equal with him. When you come across an inferior person, turn inwards and examine yourself." *The Analects,* trans. Raymond Dawson (Oxford: Oxford University Press, 1993), 14.

chapter of Luke (verses 11–32) and is commonly known as the story of the prodigal son. In both instances, certain characters make assumptions based on permanent views they have, causing them negative emotions. Christ, like the Buddha, shows that shedding such views is the key to happiness and peace.

The parable of the laborers in the vineyard goes like this: A vineyard owner needed to hire some workers for the day, so early in the morning he went into town and hired several men to work for "a penny." A few hours later, at six o'clock, the owner returned to town and hired a few more guys. He did the same at nine and at eleven. When the workday was over and it was time to pay his hired hands, the owner gave each a penny. The men who had arrived first were incensed that the workers who had arrived later, and some only after eleven, were given the same wage as they had received.

The vineyard owner responded that he did "no wrong: didst thou not agree with me for a penny? Take that thine is, and go thy way: I will give unto this last as even unto thee. Is it not lawful for me to do what I will with mine own? Is thine eye evil, because I am good?"[15] In other words, the vineyard owner is saying, "Hey, bud, you agreed early this morning to work for a penny, just as the others who arrived later did. Are you saying that you think the agreement you and I reached is unfair because of what happened afterward? You didn't say anything at the time. So take your money as we agreed and scram!"

The workers who had arrived first were perfectly willing to work all day for a penny when day broke. They had accepted their employer's offer, and everything was copacetic. Why, then, did the agreed-upon wage upset them when it came time to receive their due and proper? What had changed about the original agreement and the situation in which these early birds found themselves? Nothing! Nothing had changed for *them*. The early worker's "eye [is] evil, because [the owner is] good." Here again we see the problems that duality causes. Only when others arrived did these men think "that they should have received more"[16] than what had been promised them, and they "murmured against the goodman of

---

[15] Matthew 20:13–15 (AV).
[16] Matthew 20:10 (AV).

the house, saying 'these last have wrought but *one* hour, and thou has made them equal unto us, which have borne the burden and heat of the day.'"[17]

The text gives away the answer to the root of the problem: the early birds' perceptions. They believed that *more work equals more money*. They saw it proportionately, while the vineyard owner held fast to the original agreement. Who is right? Is it not true that people in certain professions work longer hours and earn less than those who work fewer? Is it not true that a salaried employee, whose wage is also usually predetermined by a contract, may have to work overtime and not be compensated the same way an hourly employee is? If both of these can be true, does it not also follow that more work does not always necessarily lead to greater compensation?

If the early birds understood and accepted these truths in their hearts, would they have cause for agitation and strife with their employer? Is it not so that the truth of the situation contradicted what they believed in their hearts? That was ultimately the cause of their suffering in this story—not the vineyard owner's behavior, but rather the gap between what *is* and what one *wishes to be*. The vineyard owner did exactly as he said he would and paid the promised wages without any argument. The wrong, permanent views of the workers caused their own suffering.

I've been in this very situation. Some years ago, I worked for an academic publisher, and it was my responsibility to design and build online homework assignments for college history courses. There were two historians on staff: myself, with one year of college teaching experience and a master's degree, and another historian, with a PhD and more years in the classroom under his belt. My colleague and I had the same title, but he had the word *Senior* in front of his, and he earned about 20 percent more money than I did. This pattern held true for other teams in the company as well: biology, economics, accounting, statistics, and so on.

Over time, some of the other non-"senior" developers were promoted to that level, but even after about five years, I was not. It

---

[17] Matthew 20:11–12 (AV).

began to get under my skin. Like many of them, I had contributed to the creation of a team and designed the groundwork of its product. The company hired us around the same time. My team's product was selling more or less as well as the others measured against expectations. I became annoyed that I was not getting my due, despite being paid according to the contract I had signed.

Yet, there were other factors involved. My team had undergone more management changes than others, and therefore, I didn't have a stable relationship with my superiors, as some of my colleagues did. There had been some issues with my team's budget. I wasn't as collegial of a coworker in those days as some of the others were. So, if my situation was different, why did I expect to be treated the same and given the same rewards as members of other teams? I was angry, but the anger was my fault. I held fast to the idea that I should have been treated the same as my colleagues in terms of salary and title, but was I not compensated as promised? Was the situation on my team not different? It was holding fast to expectations of how things *should have been* rather than assessing and accepting how they actually *were* that caused me the same suffering felt by those vineyard workers in Christ's story.

Christ's parable of the prodigal son as told in the sixteenth chapter of Luke is a little more widely known. In this story, there is a wealthy farmer with two sons. The older son is responsible, hardworking, and does everything his father asks of him. The younger son asks for his inheritance early, moves to the city, and squanders all that he has received on fast living. One day, the younger son feels remorse for his evil actions and decides to return to his father in shame, begging his father's forgiveness and asking to be hired as a common servant in the household.

However, the father is overjoyed by his son's return. He gives his son some flashy new clothes and slaughters the best calf on the farm for a celebratory feast. Meanwhile, the older son complains that though he had never left the farm, squandered any wealth, and so on, his father had never thrown him and his friends a fiesta with food and drink. The father chastises the older son, saying "thou art ever with me and all I have is thine. It was meet that we should make merry, and be glad: for this thy brother was dead and is alive again; and was lost, and is found."[18]

In other words, the older brother was upset that he wasn't rewarded for his steady devotion with the kind of festivity that awaited his deadbeat brother just for coming home after ending his bender. At first glance, he seems to have a point! How would you react in such circumstances? I was always a top student in my youth, yet I sometimes found that lesser students would receive more praise for accomplishments that seemed to me rather pedestrian than I would receive for doing something far more advanced.

Why did other students receiving praise disturb me? Upon revisiting the story of the prodigal son, I realized the problem. I was just like the older brother! I shared his same permanent view. Like he did, I believed that greater accomplishment and devotedness to one's work merited celebration. Yet, do not other things also merit praise? Does a student who has been struggling not gain more from praise than a student who is consistently excellent? (My subsequent experience as a teacher has made it clear that this is indeed often though, of course, not always the case.) Would a father surprised by the sudden appearance of a son he thought lost not spark joy in his heart and cause him to want to celebrate?[19] Does celebrating someone else *necessarily* have *anything* to do with me *at all*? Why am I making this about me? And most importantly, why do I think that the things *I* do are more worthy of praise than what others do? Should my standards apply to everyone? Do I like it when others measure me by their standards?[20]

The Buddha taught that the desire to remain constant and hold on to such permanent certainties as "hard work should be rewarded above all else" is the source of suffering in this world. It certainly was to the older brother in Christ's story! Similarly, wishing for our impermanent bodies to last causes suffering. Our bodies change constantly, decay, and ultimately perish. Every human has but one of two options: a quick, likely painful death, or

---

[18] Luke 16:32 (AV).

[19] Am I not sometimes happier to see my goofball five-year-old nephew than my more intellectually stimulating friends? Yes. Yes, I am.

[20] No.

the slow, drawn out decay of sickness and age. All of us, without exception, will face one of those two eventualities sooner or later. Therefore, why do we wish things to be otherwise? Why do we fear the inevitable? Can fear keep death away? What effect does holding on to life and fearing death have but creating a fearful life?

Therefore, Buddhists strive to accept their deaths in their hearts (it behooves one to remember at this juncture that the Thai word for *to understand*, เข้าใจ (pronounced KHAO-chai), translates as "to enter the heart,") and that life and death, like everything else, are dualistic in nature. To accept one is to accept the other. Since death is generally undesirable and difficult to accept, many people seek to escape it. This means renouncing life. The Buddha declined to state exactly what Nirvana is like in an experiential way as some prophets have described their heavens, but he did say that Nirvana is the unconditioned state, where duality no longer exists. It is beyond life and death. Those who accept and seek life (and death) can therefore not reach it. That is why it is so important to consider happiness and sadness, up and down, pain and pleasure, life and death as intricately bound. It is in this way that we can let go of our desires for them and thereby remove wrong, permanent views that do not conform to truth from our hearts.

There is something Christ said that never made sense to me when I was a practicing Lutheran but began to become clear after I became a Buddhist. "If any man come to me, and he hate not his father, and mother, and wife, and children, and brethren, and sisters, yea, and his own life also, he cannot be my disciple."[21] When I was a churchgoing youth, I never once heard the pastor say that I had to hate my family and my own life to be a Christian. In fact, it was quite the contrary. He always told me to love my neighbor as myself, honor my father and mother, and so on. Love and charity of both body and heart are cornerstones of Christianity. I have, in my capacity as a teacher at a Catholic school, heard many sermons given by priests and Christian laypeople, and the vast majority emphasize the importance of love as a foundational virtue. Yahweh "so loved the world that he gave his only begotten

---

[21] Luke 14:26 (AV).

Son, that whosoever believeth in him should not perish, but have everlasting life."[22]

Yet, in light of the Dharma, Luke 14:26 begins to make sense. Only one who has overcome attachment, desire, and yearning for this world, to the things of this world, to the people of this world, and indeed their own flesh can truly make their way beyond, to Heaven or Nirvana. The Gospel of Thomas[23] repeats Luke 14:26 nearly verbatim and immediately afterwards quotes Christ as saying, "Whosoever has come to know the world has discovered a carcass, and of that person the world is not worthy."[24] Christ clearly equated life with death and often emphasized the importance of giving away one's goods, of simple living, humility, and charity, for "it is easier for a camel to go through the eye of a needle, than for a rich man to enter into the kingdom of God"[25]. Nonattachment to physical goods and an eye on something better is the core of Christ's teaching. The human body is nothing more than a physical good. It is only what we carry in our hearts regarding the body that makes us afraid to lose it.

Verse 147 of the Dhammapada illustrates the Buddhist attitude toward the physical body. It reads: "Look at this dressed up body, a mass of sores, supported (by bones), sickly, a subject of many thoughts (of sensual desire). Indeed, that body is neither permanent nor enduring."[26] The Buddha spoke this in reference to a beautiful courtesan named Sirima, with whom all the men in town were in love or lust, including a Buddhist monk. The Buddha wanted to use the opportunity to teach the monk (and anyone else who cared to learn) a lesson about the physical body, so when Sirima died, the Buddha asked the king to display her body openly for some time after her death. A few days later, the Buddha went to the palace for alms and brought the lovesick monk, who was unaware that Sirima had died, with him. They arrived to see her body, rotting and putrid, lying under the sun. By the instructions of

---

[22] John 3:16 (AV).

[23] The Gospel of Thomas is one of several accounts of the life of Jesus Christ that the pagan Roman emperor Constantine declined to include in the canonical Bible at the Council of Nicaea in 325 CE.

[24] Martin Meyer, trans., The Gospel of Thomas (San Francisco: Harper, 1992), 45.

[25] Mark 10:25 (AJ).

[26] Valerie J. Roebuck, trans., The Dhammapada (London: Penguin, 2010), 31.

the Buddha, one of the attendants let it be known that any man in town could have her for a night for 1,000 coins. When nobody accepted the offer, he lowered the price to 500, 250, and finally 0.

Of course, nobody wanted to sleep with Sirima now that she was dead! Once life leaves the body, it becomes useless no matter how beautiful, fit only to burn or bury. The Buddha's lesson is clear. We must look upon all material things, including ourselves, just like the carcass of Sirima. Only then will the world not be worthy of us. Christ echoes this very sentiment shortly after saying that one must hate one's own life to follow him in Luke, saying, "Salt is good: but if the salt has lost his savor, wherewith shall it be seasoned? It is neither fit for the land, nor yet for the dunghill; but men cast it out."[27] Christ believed this so strongly that he was prepared to die to illustrate this principle, which is exactly what he did. Having considered Christ's life, let us now consider the message of his death.

---

[27] Luke 14:33–4 (AV).

Chapter 5: That Which You Are, I Was

The Rijksmuseum in Amsterdam is my favorite art museum in the entire world. There are many excellent reasons to visit this museum; here one can see some of the most famous works of world-renowned artists such as Rembrandt, Vermeer, Brueghel, and Van Gogh. I spent an entire afternoon several years ago perusing its many beautiful works of art, but the painting that remains burned into my memory is not one of the gallery's most famous. It is a small painting in a row with many others, almost an afterthought of the Northern Renaissance, and I cannot remember the name of the artist nor the painting.

Yet, I cannot forget the image. The scene is of a funeral. Gathered around the still-uncovered grave is a group of people, presumably the friends and relatives of the deceased, and a Christian clergyman performing funeral rites. There are words coming from the dead man's mouth, which translate to "That which you are, I was. That which I am, you will become."

This work of art is incredibly elegant, simple, and powerful. Rather than a traditional funerary message, which often asks mourners to hold fond memories of the deceased, pray for their soul, or offer condolences to kin, this piece invites one to internalize the concept of death and contemplate its inevitable arrival. The Buddha often exhorted his listeners to observe the dead and draw internal parallels between the corpse on display and one's own body; the story of Sirima from the last chapter is a perfect example of this. Confronting and accepting death, one's own impermanence, is the central quest of human life. The ability to เข้าใจ one's own mortality is the door to Enlightenment, and the ability to face it fearlessly with a clean conscience is the key to opening it. This is exactly the lesson that Jesus Christ attempted to teach us by his crucifixion.

Christ's torture and death on the cross is the central event in Christian theology, a singular moment that both fulfilled ancient biblical prophecy and also opened the door of Paradise to humanity. According to Christian teachings, no human ever entered Paradise until Christ's death. There are two concepts that need clarification to fully understand this principle: Jewish sacrificial practices and original sin.

The first is relatively easy to explain. In the Hebrew Bible, Jews, like their pagan neighbors, often sacrificed animals or other valuables to atone for various transgressions. There are numerous well-known examples of this. It was out of jealousy of Yahweh's satisfaction with Abel's sacrifice of a sheep and dissatisfaction with Cain's offer of grain that Cain killed his brother in Genesis 4. When Yahweh demanded that Abraham sacrifice his son, Isaac, in Genesis 23, Abraham did not question the practice itself, however perturbed he might have been at Yahweh's choice of victim. When Yahweh relented, Abraham unquestioningly sacrificed a ram instead.

This is why Christians often call Christ *agnus dei, qui tollis peccata mundi*, or the "lamb of god, who takes away the sins of the world."[28] Christians don't generally engage in animal sacrifice, as they believe that Christ's death fulfilled all of Yahweh's sacrificial needs for all of eternity, and that those who are grateful for Christ's sacrifice may take part in its merit. Christ's death covers the price of all sin to those who recognize and feel gratitude for the gift of salvation freely given by Yahweh to humanity.

Original sin, also called the "sin of Adam," is essentially mankind's primordial defiance of Yahweh's will, as symbolized by Adam and Eve eating the apple from the Tree of Knowledge. According to Christian theology, all people are born tainted with this sin so that even those who live exemplary lives cannot achieve Paradise on their own merit. Only faith in Christ's sacrifice can remove this blemish, which is washed away with baptismal water alone. This, incidentally, is why the concept of the virgin birth is so essential to Christianity; since Christians believe Christ was conceived without sexual union, he himself was not tainted with original sin.

Christians believe that during the three days between his death and resurrection, Christ visited Limbo, the first circle of Hell that contains the virtuous deceased, and brought faithful Jews (and *only* them; all others remained and, according to Catholicism, Limbo remains the postmortem destination of virtuous

---

[28] John 1:29 (AV).

non-Christians, including Jews, who remain tainted with original sin) to Paradise.[29] These became the first people to enter Yahweh's kingdom, and its gates have subsequently been open to all who accept Christ's sacrifice on their behalf.

Most Christians also believe that Christ is one person within the triune God. That is to say that Yahweh has three distinct aspects: Father (Yahweh), Son (Christ), and Holy Spirit. Each has a different function: creator, savior, and inspiration, respectively. In this view, Christ is part of Yahweh and so *knew* that, upon his death, he would return to Paradise and reassume his rightful place in the Empyrean. In other words, many people fear death because it is impossible to definitely *know* what awaits them afterward. On the other hand, Christians believe that Christ knew for a fact that there is indeed an afterlife and, moreover, knew what it is like and could be assured of his own elevated place within it.

By that logic, Christ needed not to have feared death at all. And yet, he did! According to all four canonical Gospels, in the hours before the Jewish authorities arrested him, Christ went to the Garden of Gethsemane to pray. He asked Yahweh to spare him the violent death he knew was coming, saying, "O my father, if it be possible, let this cup pass from me,"[30] "Father, all things are possible unto thee; take away this cup from me,"[31] or "Father, if thou be willing, remove this cup from me."[32] Christ's prayer asking Yahweh to change his plans and not make him go through what he knew was coming indicates that Christ, too, had at least some level of fear, if not for the fate of his eternal soul, then at least of the massive amount of physical pain that lay in store for him.

Later, when questioned both by Jewish authorities led by the high priest Caiaphas and the Roman governor of Judea, Pontius Pilate, all four canonical Gospels depict Jesus as calm, deferent, and accepting of his fate. He does not try to talk his way

---

[29] Inhabitants of Limbo, while in Hell, are not tormented or tortured. According to Dante, Limbo is a pleasant garden and represents the pinnacle of human reason and expression. The only punishment those in Limbo face is the absence of the divine presence and of hope for Paradise.

[30] Matthew 26:39 (AV).

[31] Mark 14:36 (AV).

[32] Luke 22:42 (AV).

out of trouble, even when sentenced to death quite unjustly,[33] but instead exhorts his judges to ask those whom he has taught about him and to examine their own consciences. As always, he directs those around him to turn inward to find the truth. When sentenced to death, Christ calmly and patiently endures torture, mutilation, crucifixion, and execution.

How was Christ able to maintain his composure in the face of these evils merely hours after expressing fear in his prayers? The Gospels offer a clue. After asking Yahweh to take away the cup of suffering he is about to drink, he says, "If this cup may not pass away from me, except I drink it, thy will be done,"[34] or "the cup which my Father hath given me, shall I not drink it?"[35] Christ seems to accept his fate by the end of his night in Gethsemane. It is this acceptance that allows him to calmly endure his trial, torture, and execution. In other words, Christ เข้าใจ life and death. He knew that there was no avoiding what was to come. Once he accepted that life and death were two sides of the same thing and that he, like all other people, could not escape it, he no longer had any fear of it but sought to meet it head on, get it over with, and move forward.

In other words, Yahweh has given *all of us* the cup of death. Shall we not drink it? Does it make any sense to fear what one cannot avoid? When I was in graduate school, I was very anxious about turning in my master's thesis. I knew that once I turned it in, I would be judged on it, and I wanted as much time as I could to make it better and better. I knew that sooner or later, it had to be finished, yet I stalled as much as I could, believing that the more time I spent on it, the better it would be (which is, of course, itself a fallacy; overanalysis of something can actually make it worse!). The due date eventually came, and I realized that I could not push

---

[33] Pilate found "no fault" in Christ and was very reluctant to sentence him to death. Being clever, he offered the assembled crowd the choice to free the infamous murderer Barabas or Jesus, thinking that it would be an easy and obvious choice. Pilate was shocked when the crowd, egged on by the Jewish religious authorities who felt threatened by Christ's teachings, instead bade him to free Barabas and condemn Jesus to death.

[34] Matthew 26:42 (AV).

[35] John 18:11 (AV).

it back any further. The end was unavoidable. Once this sunk in, I did what I could, turned in the thesis, and moved on. It was *over*.[36]

So it is with life and death! The day of one's death is like a deadline for a project; it has to come sooner or later. All that has a beginning has an end; all that is born must die. This is a universal truth. Acceptance of death, and proper conduct leading up to it, removes fear. There are many stories about the Buddha in which he was able to help people realize this. One of my favorites is about a weaver's daughter. She spent her days among thread, needles, spools, and fabrics, contemplating these things as she worked.

One day, she went to listen to the Buddha when he came to speak in her town. He compared life to spools of thread; some are large and take a long time to run out, some are small and run out quickly, and others are somewhere in the middle. Every kind eventually runs out, though, no matter how much thread is wound around the spool. The girl was able to internalize and เข้าใจ this teaching and accept that her life, too, was limited like thread on a spool. Some people live many years, some but a few, and some a medium number. There was as little she could do to prevent her death as she could do to prevent a spool from running out of thread when she was weaving. It was this acceptance that led her to achieve the level of *sotapanna*, or stream enterer, the first stage of Enlightenment.[37] This story inspired verse 174 of the Dhammapada, which reads: "Blind are the people of this world: only a few in this world see clearly. Just as only a few birds escape from the net, so also, only a few get to the world of the devas, and *Nirvana*."[38]

---

[36] I got an A-, so I needn't have worried.

[37] The Buddha taught that there are four stages, and each comes with the relinquishing of attachment to a certain set of worldly concerns: A *sotapanna* no longer has attachment to physical things, including their own body. A *sakadagami* is no longer concerned with status. An *anagami* has eliminated their attachments to other people. An *arahant*, or a fully enlightened person, has no more attachments whatsoever and is bound for Nirvana upon death. The Buddha was one such as these, but hardly the only one. It is not necessary to go in order; one may go from nothing to *arahant* in a single moment, but there is no going backward once one has attained a stage of Enlightenment.

[38] Valerie J. Roebuck, trans., *The Dhammapada* (London: Penguin, 2010), 36.

Christ accepted that life and death in this world come as a pair. There was no arguing that point, and Christ's human body had to die sooner or later, for Yahweh had created humans to be mortal and, as Christ admitted when praying to Yahweh, he accepted that "thy will be done." Once he accepted the mortality of his body, it became irrelevant whether the thread of his life came from a fat spool (which would take a long time to run out) or a narrow one. It would happen eventually, and he could neither control nor choose the day of his death any more than the rest of us can, for humans can know "neither the day nor the hour[39]" of their deaths.

Christ was also able to face death bravely because his heart was clean. Christians believe that Christ, being of one substance with Yahweh, was incapable of sin and lived a perfect life. Even many non-Christians agree that Christ lived an exemplary life and should be considered a remarkable human. Muslims consider him a prophet, and some Hindus even venerate him as an avatar of Vishnu![40]

What is there to fear at the moment of one's death if one has no regrets? Buddhists (and Hindus) believe in something called karma, which is best translated as "cause and effect." One's actions in this life lead to consequences in this life and in subsequent rebirths. Both moral and immoral actions will provoke a proportionate counteraction; even Sir Isaac Newton suggested the same in his third law of motion! (He was, of course, discussing the physical world, but the principle remains the same. Did not Einstein make clear that matter and energy are one substance? What is the mind if not electrical energy?) However, Buddhists and Hindus don't believe that there is some kind of eternal scorekeeper, that a god keeps track of one's deeds and doles out blessings and punishments accordingly, as Jews, Christians, and Muslims do. Deeply rooted feelings regarding one's actions, be they guilty or rightfully proud, direct the mind to the postmortem

---

[39] Matthew 25:13 (AV).

[40] Incidentally, Krishna, an avatar of Vishnu, alludes to a similar concept of the "cup of death" while alleviating Arjuna's conscience regarding killing his relatives in the *Bhagavad-Gita*, saying that he, too, had condemned all humans to death and that it is therefore impossible for Arjuna to "kill" anyone. All humans are immediately doomed at the moment of their birth.

destination one feels one *deserves*. Remember at this point what I wrote in chapter 2 regarding Virgil's assessment of how souls are damned in Dante's *Inferno*; Virgil explains that the damned do not see their fates as torturous. Yahweh created Hell as an act of divine love in order to give wicked people exactly what they want. In effect, the damned *choose* Hell, which is very congruent with the dharmic idea of karma.

By living a (by all accounts) perfect life, Christ was able to face death without any overriding feelings of guilt or shame. He accepted that death was unavoidable. He knew he had lived life in a truthful, moral, and upright manner and so, despite his fears, was able to accept his death knowing that he had no sins for which he had to pay. In this way, he could be assured of a good rebirth (in Paradise) even if he *weren't* the second member of the Trinity. I believe this is the root of the Christian belief that Christ's death saved sinners from Hell. Christ showed his followers how to live correctly and, as a result, how to face death bravely. If one can imitate Christ's life and learn from his death, they need not have fear of Hell. His life and death are blueprints for us to follow. As he himself said, "In the world ye shall have tribulation: but be of good cheer; I have overcome the world."[41] And so can we if we truly เข้าใจ the dualistic nature of life and death and live accordingly, as Christ did. Accepting the impermanent nature of one's own life leads one to conclude that there is nothing in this world worth holding onto and that doing so condemns one to the cycle of birth and death.

That which all the dead were, you are, and that which they are, you will become. There is no escaping this reality as long as one is born into this world. Deal with it, just as Christ did. He gave his life to show you how.

---

[41] John 16:33 (AV).

Chapter 6: Lord, Make Me Pure, but Not Yet!

When I was growing up in Illinois, my family lived walking distance from a shopping center. There was nothing special or unique about this particular shopping center; it could have been any one of thousands in suburban America at that time. Yet, in contrast to kids from other parts of town, I considered myself fortunate to live near it for two main reasons: first, after a short walk through the parking lot, one would arrive at a beautiful park complete with a lake and a beach, and second, it gave us kids a place to go outside of our subdivision before we were old enough to drive. I felt sorry for the kids from the other side of town, a large residential zone. Those kids faced a long walk or bike ride to get to any kind of commercial area.

So even though the local shopping center wasn't great shakes, at least it was *something*. Because it was close and very cheap, my friends and I would regularly walk to Taco Bell. Getting a snack was only one reason. Sometimes we would skate in the parking lot, sometimes we (or perhaps my parents) needed a break from band practice in the basement, and other times my friends and I just wanted some fresh air and it was a convenient destination. At any rate, I was a frequent customer.

This particular Taco Bell had a self-serve soda machine. One would purchase a cup at the counter and then fill it with whatever appealed. If one merely wanted water, the cashier would provide a small cup free of charge upon request. One day, when I was about twelve or thirteen, I had what I thought was a flash of genius. I got the idea to ask for a water cup and fill it with soda. I thought it was the perfect crime; who would bother to observe me as I filled the cup?

As it turns out, the answer was "the manager on duty at the time." Within seconds, he caught me and scolded me thoroughly. He said he was well within his right to call the police, told me that legal trouble would follow me for the rest of my life, and asked me if a criminal record was worth a Pepsi that cost something like one dollar. I was ashamed and terrified. The manager agreed to let me off with a talking-to but warned that if I ever did this again, he wouldn't be so lenient. I was lucky (and thankful) that he was more interested in teaching me a lesson than in upholding the "shoplifters will be prosecuted to the fullest extent of the law" sign in the window.

The funny thing is that this happened about a quarter of a century ago and I remember it as if it were yesterday. I have never forgotten the shame of this moment, and since that day, I've never intentionally stolen anything. This is exactly the kind of sin that Christians suppose would be wiped from my "record." Though I did wrong, I felt contrition, apologized, and have never knowingly done that thing again. It follows that I am a "good person," and even though I erred, by admitting that I was wrong and resolving to do better, I showed my inherent moral quality, for "every good tree bringeth forth good fruit; but a corrupt tree bringeth forth evil fruit. A good tree cannot bring forth evil fruit, neither can a corrupt tree bring forth good fruit. Every tree that bringeth not forth good fruit is hewn down, and cast into the fire. Wherefore by their fruits ye shall know them."[42]

The law of karma teaches otherwise. Every volitional action is like a marble let loose upon a downwardly angled plane. It does not stop merely because one regrets letting it loose; it will continue moving until the energy propelling it forward has run out or has somehow changed. If you like, it remains "of uniform motion in a right line, unless it is compelled to change that state by forces impressed thereon."[43] So, it is good that I haven't created any more negative karma in regard to theft, but that does not erase my action. The marble I rolled that day is still moving, and the fact that I haven't forgotten it is proof of that. Someday, I will have to account for this guilt and pay the price (if I haven't already somehow).

Years later, when I was about thirty-three, I read St. Augustine's Confessions for the first time. Though I had ceased to be a Christian many years prior, I read it with vigor and remain very fond of this book. I recognized so much of myself in Augustine's words. For example, in Book Two, Augustine writes of an experience very reminiscent of mine at Taco Bell. When he was

---

[42] Matthew 7:17–20 (AV).
[43] Sir Isaac Newton, *Newton's Principia: The Mathematical Principles of Natural Philosophy*, trans. Andrew Motte (New York: Daniel Adee, 1846), 83.

sixteen, he and some friends stole pears "attractive neither to look at nor to taste"[44] but not because he needed them: "Of what I stole I already had plenty, and much better at that, and I had no wish to enjoy the things I coveted by stealing, but only to enjoy the theft itself and the sin."[45] "If any part of one of those pears passed my lips, it was the sin that gave it flavour."[46]

Augustine wrote *Confessions* when he was nearly fifty years old, meaning that about thirty years had passed since the day he stole those pears. Yet he never forgot that moment of youthful indiscretion, and worst of all, still felt guilty about his motives. As I read his words, I knew exactly how he felt. How can someone be forgiven who has not yet forgiven themself? If Christ bought you tickets to see your favorite band out of the goodness of his heart but you could not for whatever reason accept the gift, could you get into the concert? Is it easy to accept a gift for which you do not feel worthy?

The part of *Confessions* I think about very frequently isn't a single incident, though, but rather one of the overarching themes that permeates Augustine's narrative. For much of his life, Augustine had not been a Christian as his mother was. Like his father, Augustine was a devotee of Greco-Roman philosophy. He studied, and later taught, the Greek and Latin classics and in this way made his living. He wasn't a particularly immoral man, but he describes himself as having a single vice—women. Augustine loved sex. According to Greco-Roman moral codes, there was nothing inherently wrong with this. Greeks and Romans of that time were generally Dionysian in their approach to sex, compared to the more Apollonian attitudes of the Christian Church, which, by Augustine's time in the fifth century CE, had been the official religion of the Roman Empire for about one hundred years.

Augustine began to study Christian theology and the Bible with Saint Ambrose of Milan and, as time went on, felt increasingly drawn to the faith. By the time he was in his thirties, the draw was irresistible. He knew in his heart that he had to reject his old life

---

[44] Augustine of Hippo, *Confessions,* trans. R. S. Pine-Coffin (London: Penguin, 1961), 47.
[45] Augustine, 47.
[46] Augustine, 49.

and become reborn in Christ. Yet he could not! He knew what he had to do but was not quite ready to give up sex. He writes, "I had prayed to you for chastity and said 'Lord, make me pure, but not yet!' For I was afraid that you would answer my prayer at once and cure me too soon of the disease of lust, which I wanted satisfied, not quelled."[47]

Later he confesses, "I was in torment, reproaching myself more bitterly than ever as I twisted and turned in my chain. I hoped that my chain might be broken once and for all, because it was only a small thing that held me now. All the same, it held me. . . . In my heart I kept saying, 'let it be now, let it be now!' and merely by saying this I was on the point of making the resolution. . . . I could almost grasp it. But I did not reach it. I could not reach out to it or grasp it, because I held back from the step by which I should die to death and become alive to life. My lower instincts, which had taken firm hold of me, were stronger than the higher. . . . I was held back by mere trifles, the most paltry inanities, all my old attachments"[48] and further, "I kept crying, saying 'How long shall I go on saying "tomorrow, tomorrow"? Why not now? Why not make an end to my ugly sins at this moment?'"[49]

Upon reading these words, my mind immediately turned to my own struggles to accept what I know is right. I know in my mind that all life ends in death. I know that when this body dies, it will no longer be mine. I know that I cannot control sickness, aging, and death. I am aware of the transience of my own existence and that to wish to continue to exist *in perpetua* in this form is not possible. I am intellectually aware of all these things, but I do not เข้าใจ them. I haven't internalized them and accepted them in my heart.

Why not? if I know they are true and my current life is not inherently satisfying. I know that changing my view of myself, letting go of my permanent, fixed views of myself, who I am, and what is mine is all that will enable me to gracefully and easily adjust when the time inevitably comes. It is as if I want to be pure, but not yet. I'm not done playing in the world yet, but it is becoming less satisfying. I see the bad that comes baked into the good, and

---

[47] Augustine, 169.

[48] Augustine, 175.

[49] Augustine, 177.

I'm beginning to เข้าใจ that they are inseparable. I ask myself every day, "How long shall I go on saying 'tomorrow, tomorrow'? Why not now? Why not make an end to my ugly sins at this moment?" When I am able to do as Augustine did and surrender to the truth that is burning inside of me and *give up hope* that I can attain true happiness in this world, then I shall be free.

St. Augustine, Sir Isaac Newton, the Buddha, and Dante Alighieri all agree: Inertia is a powerful force, and willpower is a powerful mover. It is that upon which one trains and fixates their mind that one will become; the mind goes where we send it. The Buddha taught that one's next birth will take the shape one chooses for themself, given what is available. A wise Buddhist nun once explained karma and rebirth to me in terms of going to an airport with a certain amount of money. The good karma one accumulates during their life is like money in a wallet. Imagine you arrive at the airport with $700 in your pocket and you'd like to go to Maui. However, a ticket to Maui costs $900. Paris, your second choice, is reachable for $800. For $700, you can go to Tokyo. It's not what you wanted, but sure, it'll do.

You'll enjoy it and have some fun, enjoying the bullet train, Mt. Fuji, cherry blossoms, old temples, and the modern urban jungle. But imagine all of the problems you'll encounter there: gridlocked traffic, high prices for everything, and the knowledge that you'd really just rather be in Maui. No matter what fun you have there, it isn't just what you want. You'll always find something that is less than perfect, and so you may not enjoy Tokyo all that much. However, Tokyo is what it is. It's your volition that decides that it's less than Maui. The funny thing is that no perfect destination exists, not even Maui. I love to travel and I've been to many places, but I've always found something that makes me unhappy in every place. So why do I expect perfection? Doesn't that just cause the problem in the first place?

If you have zero money, or less, you owe the airline for the cost of your flight. You have to pay in another way; that is, Hell. The major difference between Christian and Buddhist Hell is that the Buddhist variety is not eternal. Eventually, the forces that brought you there run out and change, and you will die there and be reborn somewhere else: as an animal, a demon, a human, or a god according to your level of merit.

No one state is eternal, neither hell nor the earth nor heaven. Everyone goes around in a circle, over and over, without end, until one เข้าใจ and accepts the truth, that no place will ever be worth the suffering that comes with it, that birth is not worth death, that it is impossible to have things as we want them in this universe, and then one ceases to be reborn at all. This is Enlightenment and Nirvana, beyond duality, good, and evil. Achieving this state is impossible until we cleanse our souls of all notions that things can be held constant a certain way, work the same way all the time, or are exactly as we imagine them or wish them to be. Enlightenment is not about finding happiness in the world; it is about recognizing and accepting that the world offers no happiness without sorrow attached to it and changing how we feel about the world and ourselves in our hearts, as Augustine did in his way.

In Dante's *Inferno*, the words inscribed above the Gate of Hell are:

Per me si va ne la citta' dolente,
per me si va ne l'etterno dolore,
per me si va tra la perduta gente.
Giustizia mosse il mio alto fattore:
fecemi la divina podestate,
la somma sapienza e 'l primo amore.
Dinanzi a me non fuor cose create
se non etterne, e io etterno duro.
Lasciate ogne speranza, voi ch'intrate.

[I am the way into the city of woe.
I am the way to a forsaken people.
I am the way into eternal sorrow.
Sacred justice moved my architect.
I was raised here by divine omnipotence
Primordial love and ultimate intellect
Only those elements time cannot wear
Were made before me, and beyond time I stand.

Abandon all hope, ye who enter here.][50]

They may as well be written on the interior of every eggshell and on every cervix to be read by every being born into this world. Only by giving up hope of what we *wish could be* can we perfectly accept *what is*, and yet, as Augustine so eloquently elucidates, it is the hardest thing to do.

---

[50] Dante Alighieri, *The Divine Comedy,* trans. John Ciardi (New York: New American Library, 2003), 30–31.

Section 3

The Pre-Christian Tradition

Chapter 7: The World Tree

Imagine a gigantic tree that, from its roots to its upper reaches, is as tall as the entire galaxy. Its roots extend below the great ocean, read as the vastness of space, which itself is bounded by a giant serpent called Jörmungandr. From its branches hang the nine worlds, or realms of existence: Asgard, the realm of the Æsir (higher gods)[51]; Midgard, the realm of mankind and the animals; and various others populated by beings ranging from angelic Vanir to the demonic giants called Jötnar.[52] All of these realms are interconnected by the structure of the tree itself and are dependent on its continued life.

This tree is named Yggdrasil (IG-drah-sil), also called the World Tree or the Tree of Life. Its sprouting aeons ago heralded the birth of our universe, the world system that Buddhists call *samsara*, or the system of different realms in which one can be born. Its ultimate destruction is called Ragnarök, or the twilight of the gods, when Asgard's defenders will fight a futile battle against various destructive natural forces. As stated in stanzas 44–45 of the *Völuspá* in the Poetic Edda:[53]

"Brother will fight brother and be his slayer,
sister's son will violate the kinship-bond;
hard as it is in the world, whoredom abounds,
Axe-age, sword-age, shields are cleft asunder,
Wind-age, wolf-age, before the world plunges headlong;
No man will spare another...
The ancient tree groans and the giant gets loose,

---

[51] These are equivalent to what Buddhists call the denizens of the Heaven of the Thirty-Three.

[52] These are the asuras of Hinduism and Buddhism.

[53] The Poetic and Prose Eddas are two of the few "scriptures" of pre-Christian European religion and came into existence in Iceland in the thirteenth century. Though by the time of their writing the island was officially Christian, there were still many who practiced the old faith and so the stories were well known. Icelanders wrote down what they remembered of the ancient stories in their tongue, which to this day closely resembles Old Norse, in the Poetic Edda. In addition, Snorri Sturluson wrote the Prose Edda around 1220, preserving more fragments of old pagan stories.

Yggdrasil shudders, the tree standing upright."[54]

Ragnarök is inevitable and unavoidable; Yggdrasil, like any other tree, cannot endure forever. Indeed, its decay, occurring at this very moment, is represented by the serpent Níðhöggr, who lives among the roots of the tree and constantly gnaws at them. Yggdrasil's collapse will bring about the death of this universe. However, it is important to remember that while birth is the cause of death, the converse is also true. From the ashes of Yggdrasil, a new tree will sprout, and out of it—a new *samsara* and new life.

In this most foundational of its myths, pre-Christian Northern European religion[55] expresses the cycle of birth and death in a timeless, dendritic metaphor common to other traditions we have examined. The very universe itself is subject to the incontestable law of impermanence. It is born, grows, flowers, ages, and eventually is destroyed. There is nothing the gods can do to stop this process, in the same way that there is nothing a gardener can do to stop a tree they are tending from shedding its leaves at the onset of winter. There is nothing a human being can do to stop their own aging and death.

Yggdrasil, as well as the worlds it ties together in its branches, represents the interconnectedness of the universe. Beings move between these worlds; the Æsir are able to do so by using the Bifröst, a bridge made from a rainbow that allows the gods to travel to and from Asgard. Humans can also travel between worlds, but only by passing through the portal of death. After the demise of the mortal coil, a human awakens reborn in the world that best suits their temperament in life. The virtuous and peaceful awaken in Vanaheimr, the world of the Vanir. The unremarkable go to Hel, which resembles less the Christian idea of a place where sinners are tortured than the dismal, grey realm where "people sit in darkness; dust is their food and clay their meat,"[56] which the

---

[54] Carolyne Larrington, trans., *The Poetic Edda* (Oxford: Oxford University Press, 1996), 10.

[55] I will henceforth refer to this religion as *Ásatrú*. The word itself means "loyalty to the Æsir" and is the contemporary version of the pre-Christian faith. Since very few sources remain from the pre-Christian era, modern practitioners have had to reconstruct the religion from fragments. I will use *Ásatrú* to refer to the faith because, as far as we know, this tradition had no name before Christians destroyed it. The modern iteration, in substance as well as in name, will have to suffice.

[56] N. K. Sandars, trans., *The Epic of Gilgamesh* (London: Penguin, 1960), 92.

world's oldest hero, Gilgamesh, dreaded so much that he sought eternal life on earth from Utnapishtim, the Sumerian Noah. There are realms where the violent, incontinent, and treacherous are tortured. The brave and loyal go to the most famous of the halls of Asgard, Valhalla, where they await the honor of fighting alongside Odin during Ragnarök.

The parallels to the Abrahamic afterlife that I have already discussed, largely in the context of Dante's work, are obvious. A recently deceased soul makes its way to the destination for which it has conditioned and prepared itself during life. There, it is reborn in a new body, be it of a hell being or of one of the blessed. What is less well known to most Western readers is that the Ásatrú cosmology overlaps considerably with its Hindu-Buddhist counterpart.

Just as Christ was born and raised as a Jew, Siddhartha Gautama, the man who would become the Buddha when he was thirty-five years old, began his life practicing an iteration of the religion commonly referred to in our time as Hinduism. There is therefore a lot of overlap between the Buddhist and Hindu cosmos. Generally, Buddhist teachers do not encourage practitioners to focus their attention on this topic; the Buddha avoided discussing the origin and structure of the universe and possible afterlives into which one could be reborn, preferring instead to instruct others on how to look within oneself and remove one's wrong, permanent views (called *micchā diṭṭhi)*.

However, it is my experience that Westerners, accustomed as they are to scripture, origin stories, abstract theological theories, and stories of gods, men, and god-men, often have questions along these lines when they begin to learn about Dharmic religions.[57] This seems an appropriate place to discuss these matters, if not only to appeal to the conditioned sensibilities of Western readers, then at least to draw clear parallels between the Dharmic universe and that of Ásatrú in order to demonstrate the syncretic possibilities of these traditions separated by thousands of kilometers.

---

[57] Dharmic religions include Hinduism, Buddhism, Jainism, and other religions originating in the Indian subcontinent related to these three. As a contrast, one may use the term *Abrahamic* to refer to Judaism, Christianity, Islam, Rastafarianism, and any other religion in which Yahweh plays the central role.

Buddhists and Hindus, just like Christians, Muslims, and Ásatrúar,[58] generally believe that after death, humans are reborn in destinations that reflect the mindset to which they conditioned themselves during their lives (see chapter 2 for Dante and Virgil's conversation about the willingness of the damned to take up their positions in Hell). These can range from ecstatic to incredibly torturous, depending on the nature and gravity of one's previous actions. Many Buddhists and Hindus also believe in heavens and hells, demons and angelic beings, and gods and devils (though, of course, some do not or find such things irrelevant).

There are a few key differences, though. Monotheists tend to think that humans are only born twice: once into this world, and once into either Hell, Purgatory, or Paradise. Ásatrúar agree but know that "heaven" is not eternal and that their second lives will end with Ragnarök. Buddhists and Hindus believe that humans are born (and die) an essentially infinite number of times in most, if not all, of the realms without end until achieving the ultimate goal of *moksha* (for Hindus) or Enlightenment (for Buddhists). Buddhists and Hindus seek to essentially stop being born into *any* world, be it heavenly, hellish, or somewhere in between. Removing oneself from the karmic cycle of birth is the only way to escape death, as well as more mundane forms of suffering.

Both *moksha* and Enlightenment entail removal from the cycle of rebirth, albeit under different circumstances. *Moksha* is the internalization of the fact that one is not in any way separate from other beings, especially the Great Brahman, the source of universal consciousness of which all other consciousnesses, even yours, are merely varied reflections.[59] Upon this realization, the soul is completely reabsorbed into Great Brahman and one's individual experience of the universe ceases. This presupposes the existence of *attā*, or a permanent "self," that is unique and the

---

[58] Ásatrúar are people who practice Ásatrú.

[59] Most Hindus believe that the universe is a single consciousness that expresses itself in an infinite number of ways. They call this consciousness "Great Brahman," in essence another way to say "God." All beings are reflections of certain aspects of the infinite nature of divine consciousness. In other words, God is infinite, and in order for infinity to exist, all possible iterations of reality *must* exist. That explains the unending variety of beings in the world, and why you are you in all of your unique beauty and glory. You express the part of God that looks, acts, sounds, and so on the way you do, as all beings must. In that way you are both you and part of God.

essence of each being, or if you like, Kant's concept of the *Ding an sich*. (For more on this, see the *Bhagavad Gītā*, particularly chapters 2, 4, and 7.)

Buddhists approach awakening another way, through the Buddha's teaching of "not-self"—*anattā*. 'Self' is merely a self-induced delusion, created the same way that the mind creates the concept of 'house' from its elements, as I discussed in chapter 2 of this book while referencing Sariputta's speech in the Greater Discourse of the Elephant's Footprint in the Majjhima Nikāya. Enlightenment, or reaching Nirvana, occurs when one เข้าใจ this misunderstanding and simply ceases to exist. Accordingly, *nirvana* translates to "snuffing out."

Hindus believe that the three top-level gods are Brahma the Creator, Vishnu the Preserver, and Shiva the Destroyer. In many ways, each of these deities represents a different part of the natural life cycle: birth, life, and death, respectively. The fact that their existence is foundational means that all life is based on their natures. Since birth and death are essentially beyond all alteration and what comes between is variable, many Hindus choose to worship Vishnu. It is Vishnu's job to maintain peace, order, 'goodness,' and the proper working of the universe so that it may see out its lifespan. If Brahma makes the car and Shiva junks it, then Vishnu is the mechanic who keeps it running.

Vishnu is also the deity who intervenes in the world most frequently. Hindus believe that he has been born as a man six times, and many believe that the Buddha is one of those incarnations. The two most famous incarnations of Vishnu are Krishna and Rama. As Krishna, Vishnu was a spiritual teacher who attempted to convince mankind to create balance on its own. The Hindu *Bhagavad Gītā* features Krishna's conversation with a hero named Arjuna, whose family had become a bunch of jerks and were perpetrating evil acts. Krishna attempts to convince Arjuna to fight and slay his evil family in battle, arguing that since the soul is immortal, Arjuna isn't really killing them but merely sending them to their next lives, preserving order and goodness in the world along the way. In other words, Krishna passes on to Arjuna the cup that Yahweh handed to Christ.

In the Hindu Rāmāyana, Vishnu is born as a man named Rama primarily to fight the demon king Ravana, who was bringing disorder and evil into the world. Among other sins, Ravana kidnapped Rama's wife, Sita, and imprisoned her in his lair on Sri Lanka. Their battle represents a struggle between good and evil, or if you prefer, truth and delusion, in which Rama was victorious due in large part to the aid of the lesser god Hanuman and his monkey army. The Rāmāyana is an important foundational story throughout not only India but also all of Southeast Asia; for example, images from the story decorate the walls of the Royal Palace complex in Bangkok, Thailand.

Both of these stories of Vishnu on earth read as victories of good over evil, of order over chaos. They are predicated on the notion of the preservation not only of the world but also the people in it and of 'goodness.' In many ways, they represent the tendency of mankind to see life as good. Ásatrúar agree with this on a deep, fundamental level. The Æsir often make great personal sacrifices to preserve life in *samsara* (see chapters 8 and 10). Odin gathers the bravest and strongest warriors slain on the battlefield and takes them to Valhalla in order to prepare them for the final battle at Ragnarök. He engineers wars so as to gather more soldiers and train them properly in his hall. Like Vishnu, Odin keeps the big picture in mind, opting at times to sacrifice individual people in order to preserve the cosmic order.

Yet, both Vishnu and Odin know that, ultimately, their quests are futile. Shiva will have his day and destroy the world; Vishnu knows this. The Æsir will lose the battle on the day of Ragnarök, and Yggdrasil will die; Odin knows this. The preservation of the universe for all time is a futile, Quixotic quest. The Buddha himself described the inevitable destruction (and rebirth) of *samsara*, saying in the Brahmajāla Sutta, "There comes a time . . . sooner or later after a long period when the world contracts . . . but the time comes, sooner or later after a long period, when this world begins to expand."[60] The Buddha goes on to explain how, after the world is reborn, the different heavenly, earthy, and hellish realms are filled as beings fall from higher states and after its destruction,

---

[60] Maurice Walshe, trans., *The Long Discourses of the Buddha: A Translation of the Dīgha Nikāya* (Boston: Wisdom Publications, 1987), 75.

beings ascend to higher levels until the whole process starts over again.

This all goes to show that Hinduism, Buddhism, and Ásatrú share a common conception of the universe as made up of varied realms that are both cyclical and doomed. It is impossible to hope that the structure can be maintained forever, though it is worth preserving as long as possible so that beings can learn, grow, and become awakened during times of stability in order to escape its inevitable destruction. We are given this time to become better versions of ourselves; Vishnu and Odin do their best to keep Yggdrasil alive as long as possible. It is up to us to use the time given to us. In the face of the fact that we live in a futile, doomed universe, the best way to show gratitude to the gods for their work is to do what they ask us to do: accept and เข้าใจ the impermanent, dualistic nature of the universe and the relationship between death and birth in order that we, like the Buddha, can transcend them.

When I was growing up, my family gathered around the dinner table as a group six nights out of seven. I didn't mind; I've always enjoyed spending time with my family. The topics we discussed over meals were usually heavy: politics, history, religion, world affairs, literature, and things like that. The discussions were often heated and detailed, which was possible because we all loved and respected each other regardless if we agreed or not. My father and I agreed, and still agree, on a lot of things. We overlap far more than we differ. However, my father has this infuriating habit of, as he puts it, "playing devil's advocate" and arguing the converse of whatever position I take.

The frustrating part is that I know that he doesn't actually disagree with me most of the time. When I was young, I didn't understand why he wouldn't say what he actually thought and seek harmony in our discussions, instead arguing for the mere sake of it. He said that he enjoyed engaging in debate, and years later I recognized that despite my frustrations, engaging in these discussions over time sharpened my ability to think logically and support points with evidence. This skill is useful in many situations in my life, not least because I am a historian; the historical craft centers around being able to argue one's thesis using evidence from primary and secondary sources.

I didn't know it at the time, but teaching me to think was exactly my father's goal over all of those intense dinnertime discussions. Only years later did he tell me that this had been his objective all along. He didn't want to make things easy on me; he wanted to challenge and push me to become a critical, robust thinker and eloquent speaker. I found the path he laid in front of me difficult, irritating, and winding, but in the end, I'm very thankful that he took this approach with me. Despite my feelings at the time, my father helped me develop a skill that has become essential to my professional and personal life.

This is an example of why it is important to remember that impermanence comes in many different forms. It is easy to observe physical impermanence. The buds one sees on tree branches in March become April's flowers and ultimately autumn's fruit. These debates with my father, his goals and my frustrations, demonstrate the other, intangible, variety of impermanence. Can you think of a time when something irritating, hurtful, or perhaps tragic occurred in your life? Think of what you learned from that experience or what changed as a result of it. If some benefit came from it, even much later, can this experience truly have been unequivocally bad? What I saw as annoying and difficult as a youth has blossomed into a fruitful harvest that I continue to reap in my adult life, and I am thankful for it. It is impossible to know what the results of any action, moment, or change will be in the long run. It is therefore vital that we approach each moment without certainty and preconceived notions, open to any outcome. Had I been less certain my father was just being difficult with me and more open to the possibilities of the moment, I needn't have felt as much negative emotion then as I did. Now, I can't help but laugh at that old version of myself.

This practice works with more severe suffering as well. My mother is from Austria, which means that my grandparents lived in the Third Reich. That experience, in addition to the madness of war, created deep wounds that never fully healed in my grandparent's and mom's hearts, and they often spoke of these things with me. Over time, I began to feel their pain, and as one might imagine, the topic is very sensitive to my entire family. The fact that my father is from Poland made things all the more complicated for me internally when I was young, as well as for my extended family in terms of interpersonal relationships. Let's just say there were some tense moments.

When I was in high school, math was my weakest subject. Luckily, my closest childhood friend is very good at it and often helped me understand concepts I found particularly challenging. One day, he and I were sitting in the back of the classroom as the teacher was going over something that he and I understood already. We were quietly discussing a homework problem that I didn't fully understand. My teacher was not pleased and suggested in front of the entire class and my half-Jewish best friend that if I had difficulty paying attention to the "person at the front of the room speaking," then as a person of (Austro-)German origin, I should merely "pretend that (he is) Hitler."

I've never been more mortified in my entire life. It is the one time I've ever blacked out. I don't remember my exact thoughts in the moments that followed—I went numb. I'm told I turned beet red and left the room. I didn't return to class for a few days after that. However, as badly as I felt in that moment, I resolved to never ever intentionally make someone feel ashamed of who they are or where they come from. I hadn't been inclined to do so before then either, but the raw emotion and pain of that moment helped me internalize how hurtful such things can be. I learned what it's like to be ethnically slurred, and I've been careful to be sensitive regarding the words that I use with other people.

Despite the discomfort of that moment, I am thankful that it happened, for I experienced something that many White people do not, and it has made me a better man. Understanding the impermanence of that moment makes it difficult for me to consider that moment entirely negative. In other words, the moment has no self. It was neither wonderful nor tragic. It merely was. I also try to remember that, however inelegantly he expressed it, my teacher had a point. I'm a high school teacher now, and I don't appreciate it when students engage in side conversations regardless of their content. In the end, how I interpret that experience and what I feel about it is up to me. Rather than see just one side, I try to see it for all that it was and all that it inspired.

Still, it is difficult to see beyond the moment when one is in it. This ability, or at least the willingness to work toward it, is vital for Ásatrúar who are devotees of Odin. Odin is the wisest of the gods, and sometimes, his ways are hard to understand. In order to have some idea of why this is, let's consider some basic facts about him. He is usually depicted as an old man in a wide-brimmed hat with a long white beard. He walks with a large stick, fights with a spear, and his left eye is missing. Two ravens named Huginn and Muninn accompany him. Their names translate as Thought and Memory, and each day they fly around the earth and report what they see to their master.

Odin is also called Allfather and holds the position of the highest of the Æsir. Ásatrúar consider him to be their father in the same way that Christians consider Yahweh to be theirs. But like my earthly father's, his methods don't always make sense to his children at first pass. Odin sees more than we can, and his actions, though sometimes baffling in the moment, are done with the big picture in mind. For example, because he needs warriors to train in Valhalla in preparation for Ragnarök, he engineers wars on earth so that he can reap the souls of the bravest dead. This is tragic from an earthly point of view, but in accordance with the Buddha's teachings on impermanence, it happens for an important reason that those who die, and their families, cannot fully see nor understand.

Thus, one who follows and venerates Odin must be patient and be able to have faith in one who knows and sees more than themselves. His is not an easy path. Other deities like Freyja or Thor are more suitable for an Ásatrúar whose practice necessitates more protection, love, compassion, and care. Followers of Odin must be of relatively pure moral background because pursuing wisdom regardless of the cost is difficult if one has a lot of bad karma resulting from prior unwholesome actions. Only one who has little or no bad karma to fear can readily accept some of the difficult situations, and the resulting lessons, that lead to higher levels of wisdom.

Sacrifice is essential while walking the path toward Enlightenment. Many stories of Odin revolve around him undergoing great physical torment and even death in pursuit of a higher ideal. Like Christ, Odin faced such ordeals with confidence in ultimate deliverance because he possessed wisdom and a clean heart. There are two stories about Odin that illustrate his understanding of the impermanence and suffering of the body that I'd like to discuss. The first relates to his death and rebirth while hanging from the branches of Yggdrasil in order to achieve knowledge of the Futhark runes. The second explains why Odin willingly gave up his left eye.

The *Hávamál* is a collection of the sayings of Odin that makes up part of the Poetic Edda. Odin describes his death while hanging from Yggdrasil in stanzas 138–42 of *Hávamál*:

"I know that I hung on a windswept tree
nine long nights
wounded with a spear, dedicated to Odin,

myself to myself
on that tree of which no man knows
from where its roots run.
With no bread did they refresh me nor a drink from a horn,
downwards I peered;
I took up the runes, screaming I took them,
then I fell back from there.
Nine mighty spells I learnt from the famous son
of Bolthor, Bestla's father,
and I got a drink of the precious mead
I soaked from Odrerir
Then I began to quicken and be wise,
and to grow and to prosper
one word from another word found a word for me,
one deed from another deed found a deed for me.
The runes you must find and meaningful letters,
very great letters,
very stiff letters,
which the mighty sage coloured,
and the huge Powers made
and the runemaster of the gods carved out."[61]

Why did he undergo such torment? Twice in this excerpt, Odin mentions the runes, that he "took up the runes, screaming," and then describes how, upon attaining them, he "began to quicken and [become] wise". What are the runes? They have two functions. Pre-Christian Germanic peoples used them as an alphabet, and in the few instances in which they would write things down, or to be more precise, carve words into stone, they wrote the text in runic script. The runes also function as a set of mystical symbols for certain metaphysical concepts that, once understood, grant great wisdom and power. It was in order to acquire this knowledge of the runes that Odin suffered his own death and resurrection.

In this way, Odin mirrors Christ in that he was willing to sacrifice his body and his life for a higher purpose. Christ became

---

[61] Carolyne Larrington, trans., *The Poetic Edda* (Oxford: Oxford University Press, 1996), 32.

the savior of mankind. Odin did as well, but less directly; he now has wisdom to share not only with his children but also to use in preparation for Ragnarök. His sacrifice exemplifies the type of understanding that it takes to reach the level of a *sotapanna*, or stream-enterer. *Sotapannas* are beings who have achieved the first level of Enlightenment. Such beings เข้าใจ the impermanence and suffering of the physical body and release all ties to it. Odin was willing to sacrifice his body to attain wisdom, which one can do only if one has severed the heart's attachment to it.

What makes the runes such powerful symbols? Let's consider an example. Each rune, just like each letter of the Roman alphabet that you are reading now, has a name. This is Nauthiz:

It represents the concepts of need, self-reliance, endurance, and renunciation. I've always understood its meaning as "where there is a need, there is less freedom." Consider a person who is self-driven to take a shower every day or feels somehow unwell if they do not. That person is far less likely to experience incredible things like hiking to the top of a mountain, camping near the summit, and bathing in the glory of nature for a few days. Someone who may enjoy a shower every day but has no such need will happily make an adjustment when necessary and shower when appropriate. Being flexible and ready to adapt opens the door to richer experiences, spontaneity, and a greater understanding of different ideas.

A need is a limitation one places on one's own freedom both of action and of thought; it functions essentially as an internal asymptote. To describe it according to a Buddhist framework, it is one of many *micchā diṭṭhi*, or wrong views. Wrong views are notions we all hold according to some permanent principle that do not hold up against the universal truth of impermanence. Creating needs in one's mind is tantamount to creating an unnecessary blockage within oneself that will create equally unnecessary suffering. The Nauthiz rune represents this entire concept in a single character. Contemplation of the runes and their meanings, like the process of examining one's emotions as I've discussed earlier, is a window into the mind[62] that enables a person to dig out their wrong views, examine them, and ideally shed them.

After obtaining understanding of the runes, Odin made them available for us to use as contemplation tools. He was willing to sacrifice his physical body to become something greater than he was and, like Christ, to show us how. But that is not the only physical sacrifice Odin has made for wisdom. He also gave up his left eye. Near the roots of Yggdrasil lies Mímisbrunnr, or the well of Mimir. The Prose Edda attests that its waters contain "wisdom and intelligence"[63] and that Odin wished to drink from it. However, the guardian of the well, Mimir, demanded payment. The Edda reads, "Allfather went there and asked for a drink from the well, but he did not get this until he gave one of his eyes as a pledge."[64] According to the Völuspá:

> "I know all about it, Odin, where you hid your eye
> in Mimir's famous well."[65]

Once again, Odin sacrificed an essential part of his body in order to become something *more*, both for his own benefit and the benefit of his children. The eye is an extremely important organ, and yet Odin did not hesitate to exchange it for a drink from the well that would give him even more wisdom. Only one who เข้าใจ the suffering and impermanence of the physical body would be ready to make that trade without hesitation. Incidentally, Christ agrees when he says, "And if thy right eye offend thee, pluck it out and cast it from thee: for it is profitable for thee that one of thy members should perish, and not that thy whole body should be cast into Hell."[66]

---

[62] Kind of like Tarot!
[63] Snorri Sturluson, *The Prose Edda,* trans. Jesse L. Byock (London: Penguin, 2005), 24.
[64] Sturluson, 24–25.
[65] Larrington, 7.
[66] Matthew 5:29 (AV).

One can apply this principle to many aspects of life. Why, while writing this book I've had to do so! When I was working out the structure of this book, I had envisioned two more chapters than there are now. I thought that those chapters were well researched and well written. However, when I contemplated the message that I am trying to send *as a whole*, I realized that they did not help all that much— so I left them out. I experienced something similar when I was recording my last album, *Various Ointments.*[67] Two songs didn't make the final cut; though I thought that each was a good track, their presence detracted from the record as a singular piece of art, so I left them out.

Odin teaches us the Dharma through his actions. He proves willing to sacrifice his physical well-being, and indeed his very life, to attain a higher level of mental and spiritual development. In this way, he is an example and a role model to which all humans can aspire. Odin cares so much for his children that he is preparing to fight a gruesome, futile battle at Ragnarök, but more than preserve this world, he wants us to learn to เข้าใจ the impermanence and suffering of the physical body, release our attachments, and join him on the path to Enlightenment. He will help you if you ask him—just don't expect him to make it easy for you!

---

[67] *Various Ointments* is available for free at www.deweysweet.com, but if you choose to donate, all proceeds go toward paying the mortgage on the Akaliko women's Dharma center at Wat San Fran Dhammaram, a Buddhist temple in San Francisco.

Chapter 9: The Bottomless Ale Horn

In February 2020, I had plans to visit Lisbon, Portugal for a week. About six months prior I had purchased plane tickets and reserved a place to stay, and as my departure date approached, I was ready to go. I was very much looking forward to visiting the city; many of my friends had said glowing things about it, and I had been studying Portuguese for nearly a year at that time. I was excited to test out my language skills and to learn even more. I had a week off from work and had made all the preparations necessary to be away from San Francisco without issue.

The day finally came—Friday, February 14. My flight was scheduled to leave around eight o'clock that evening. I calculated that I had to leave my apartment at about five o'clock. I left work at the end of the day with boundless energy. All that remained was to get home, grab my bag, and head to SFO. Yet, during my walk home, I received a text message from the airline with which I had booked my flight from London (where I was to have a short layover) to Lisbon. It turned out that there was a powerful storm battering southeastern England that day, and that flight had been canceled.

I rushed home to see what could be done to ameliorate the situation, arriving at four o'clock. That gave me about an hour to figure out what to do. By 4:45, it became clear that, for various reasons, my least-bad option was to cancel the entire trip and spend my week off in California. For a very brief moment, I was sorely disappointed. I had been so looking forward to this trip! However, my mind immediately began to contemplate the impermanence of the situation.

First of all, it's no bad thing to have a week off in San Francisco. Though I've lived here for over a decade, I always discover new secrets when I walk around, and some spots I visit infrequently. The weather forecast for the week showed sun and warmth. So far, so good. Then, I began to look a little deeper. In addition to the fact that I would be able to do a lot of good things at home that week, how could I be sure I was going to have a good time in Lisbon? Was it not possible that events could have gone badly there? I could have become injured or ill, I could have had an awkward run-in with an ex-girlfriend who lives there, perhaps I wouldn't have liked the city that much, or maybe the weather would have been terrible. Any number of misfortunes could have transpired. I realized that any disappointment on my part was my "fault" resulting from a *micchā diṭṭhi*, or wrong view—*I would have a better time there than here*. When I realized that I could not know if this were true or not, it became easy for me to commit to making the week in San Francisco the best it could be and not think about Lisbon anymore.

Even more striking is something I could not have realized at that time but shortly became painfully clear. Had I gone on this trip, I might have run into severe problems *nobody* foresaw. Just a few weeks after I was scheduled to have returned to California, the entire world locked down due to the Covid-19 pandemic. Even now, I shake my head in amazement at how timely and serendipitous it was that a storm hit London and my flight was canceled *just as I was preparing to head to the airport*. I have come to believe that this was the work of none other than Thor, the god of thunder and the protector of humanity. I'm fairly certain he sent those storms at least in part to protect me from Covid and related issues regarding the pandemic.

In our time, most people think of the version of Thor popularized by Chris Hemsworth in the Marvel Universe. What they fail to realize is that Marvel based its hero on the most famous of the Æsir. Ásatrúar have been venerating Thor for a very long time. He is the son and heir of Odin, and the mightiest and haughtiest of the gods. He wields the enchanted hammer Mjölnir as his weapon and the instrument through which he channels his power. Ásatrúar associate him with storms, trees, strength, and protection. He is an excellent god for those who feel vulnerable and in danger. Thor has a big heart and wishes for the safety of everyone, on whose behalf he has on several occasions waged war with the Jötnar.[68] It is a good idea to pray to Thor in order to ask him to watch over the physical body while one dedicates one's mind and soul to the pursuit of wisdom with his father Odin.

---

[68] The Jötnar are a race of giants that inhabit Jötunheimr, one of the worlds in the branches of Yggdrasil. Buddhists and Hindus call this race *asuras*.

In addition to his protection, we can be thankful to Thor for other reasons. His haughtiness often gets him into difficult situations. I'd like to discuss a particular one that teaches an excellent Dharma lesson. Snorri Sturluson, an Icelander who lived in the thirteenth century, relates the story in sections 46 and 47 of the *Gylfaginning*, part of the Prose Edda. One day, Thor and some of his companions arrived at the fortress of Skrýmir,[69] a Jötnar king. Before supper, Skrýmir challenged Thor and his companions to show off their special talents, saying, "No one can stay here with us who does not have some skill or knowledge greater than other men."[70]

Thor answered that he would like to pit himself against someone in drinking ale. Skrýmir arranges for a horn to be brought to Thor that "did not seem to be very large, although it was rather long." He says that Thor would impress the assembly if he could drain the horn in a single swig but that "no one is such a small-time drinker that he cannot finish it in three." Thor was "quite thirsty and began to drink, swallowing hugely and thinking that it would not be necessary to bend himself over the horn more than once. When he had drunk as much as he could, he bent back from the horn and looked in to see how much drink remained. It seemed to him that the level in the horn was only slightly lower than it had been before."[71]

Skrýmir taunted Thor, who wordlessly went in for a second drink. "He struggled with it as long as he could hold his breath and noticed that he could not lift up the bottom end of the horn as much as he would have liked. When he lowered the horn from his mouth and looked in, it seemed to him that the level had gone down even less than it had in the first try." The thunder god then took a third drink and noticed that he had failed to drain much more from the horn that time as well.

How could this be? The mightiest of the Æsir could not drain the horn in three gulps! It was not until the following morning that Skrýmir explained what had happened. He told Thor that the

---

[69] The text also refers to Skrýmir as Útgarða-Loki, but I will use the former name so that the reader does not confuse him with Loki, the Ásatrú god of mischief and trickery who is at different times both a companion and an adversary of Thor.

[70] Snorri Sturluson, *The Prose Edda*, trans. Jesse L. Byock (London: Penguin, 2005), 58.

[71] Sturluson, 59.

god would "never have been allowed to enter [Skrýmir's castle] if [he] had known in advance that [Thor] had so much power in [him]. [72]" Skrýmir went on to tell Thor that the reason he couldn't lift the back end of the horn as high as he would have liked was that it was connected to the ocean and that when Thor "come[s] to the ocean, [he] will see how much [his] drinking lowered it. This is now known as the tides." Upon hearing that he had been tricked, Thor became angry and moved to strike Skrýmir with Mjölnir, but before he could land a blow, the Jötnar king had vanished without a trace.

I've always found this story amazing for several reasons. First of all, it is hard not to marvel at the power of Thor, because even though he failed to drain the horn, he created the tides! Yet I think other lessons one can be learned from Thor's experience, two in particular from a Buddhist perspective: one involving the size of the world versus the strength of a single individual and the other related to Thor's misplaced anger when the truth became clear to him.

Regarding the first, what strikes me about the story is that the mightiest of the Æsir could make only a superficial dent in the world at large. The ocean is so vast that even Thor could barely scratch its surface with three mighty swigs. If *Thor* could change the world only a little bit, *what chance do I have*? The world is massive, complicated, and beyond the control of even the strongest of us. I am just one mortal human. Whatever change I can create in the world will be, at best, of a very small magnitude; in the scope of eternity; irrelevant; and given the limitations of my perspective, possibly horrifying.[73] My conclusion is that trying to make the world into what I want it to be is impossible and Quixotic. I'm reminded of the inscription on the gates of Dante's Hell: "Abandon all hope, ye who enter here."

Regarding the second, I think Thor was wrong to be angry when he learned the truth of what Skrýmir did. Thor was angry with Skrýmir because he was "unfairly" prevented from winning the contest. Yet when I read the story, I ask myself why Thor found it so necessary to win. That is Thor's *micchā diṭṭhi*, or wrong view:

---

[72] Sturluson, 62.

[73] A wise man once told me that "every villain is the hero of their own story." Indeed. As the old proverb suggests, "the way to Hell is paved with good intentions."

winning is essential. It's impossible to know *why* someone might find losing intolerable. There can be many reasons: one might feel that others don't respect a loser, personal insecurity may play a big role, one may enjoy a feeling of schadenfreude when vanquishing others, one may be addicted to the adrenaline rush that comes with a triumph, or any number of other reasons. It's impossible to know why Thor believed this.

What one should do when considering this story about Thor, as Confucius, Christ, and Buddha all suggest, is turn inward. I struggle with a similar wrong view that contemplation of this story brings to the surface for me. I require the respect and admiration of other people, though for my intellect rather than for strength, as is Thor's wish. It irritates and angers me greatly when I feel that others do not adequately recognize my intelligence and respect me for it. So, what assumption do I hold that makes me need this? It's something I struggle with every day. After much contemplation, I have come to know that I believe *the smartest person is the best person*. There are two layers of impermanence in that statement that I contemplate regularly: First, is that really true? Second, why do I want to be the "best person"?

There have been incredibly smart people that I would hardly call "the best." By all accounts, Alexander of Macedon (or if you prefer, Alexander the Great) was a genius. Yet he was a warmonger who was responsible for the death of untold thousands of people. Caesar, Attila, Napoleon, and others further exemplify the idea that intelligence alone does not make one "great." Merely having the capacity to learn and apply information can lead to horrifying results if not combined with humility and morality. If I constantly seek to prove my intelligence, am I not making it more difficult for myself to cultivate humility? Furthermore, have there been people of far lower levels of intellect than I who are great? Both of my grandfathers barely finished grade school, and yet they were men of incredible kindness, humility, compassion, and dedication. To me, they were great, and I consider them my heroes. So why is it that I attach such weight to intelligence and education? Is it not an (at best) incomplete and (at worst) wrong, permanent view I hold?

When I think about the second layer of impermanence, the question of why I want to be great, I return to my quest to be a professional musician or, if you like, a rock star. Forcing, manipulating, or otherwise convincing other people to see me as I want them to is very difficult. Cultivating a certain image of myself requires a huge amount of effort, including spending many of my Friday nights lugging heavy equipment up and down narrow staircases in clubs, haggling with booking guys and managers, enduring long nights, and so much more. And after all this effort, I cannot forget that the things I think are impressive may be massive turnoffs to others. To put it another way, it feels a bit like I am Thor attempting to drain the ocean. Though I may be successful among some groups of people in certain contexts, forcing the world to see me as I see myself is a Sisyphean task.

Rather than attempt to shape the world to our liking, it is incumbent on each of us to accept things as they are. As I've argued, there are two main ways to do so. One is to measure the costs against the potential benefits of working to change the world, as I did when I gave up on my dream to be a musician. The other is to contemplate the idea that the change one wants to create may not yield the desired results, or that the desired results may come with unforeseen, or horrific, side effects. Thor's need for renown, fame, respect, and recognition led him to anger; he wanted to strike Skrýmir down when the giant revealed his deception. Murder carries a heavy karmic penalty.

Instead, we must give up on the idea of changing the world, which Thor unintentionally shows us is extremely difficult at best. Looking inward and removing our wrong, permanent views of how things *must* or *should* be, abandoning hope of "fixing" the world, and dropping conditions, including the need to "win" and make things as we want them, is the path to happiness and peace. If Thor were able to do so, he may well have been able to have a laugh with Skrýmir rather than to try harming him. As thankful as I am to Thor for watching over me and preventing harm from befalling me, I am even more thankful for the opportunity to learn from his mistakes.

Just as Christians are divided between three major branches of their faith—Orthodoxy, Catholicism, and Protestantism[74]—so is Buddhism split between the Theravada, Mahayana, and Vajrayana schools. Just as Protestantism grew out of Catholicism and has a lot in common with its antecedent, so, too, is Vajrayana an offshoot of Mahayana. I have until this point written almost exclusively about Theravada approaches to Dharma for several reasons. Foremost among them is that Theravada is the interpretation of the Dharma that I personally practice and therefore feel most comfortable discussing, but I also believe it to be the most effective and direct of the schools in dealing with questions of personal suffering, which is what brought me to Buddhism in the first place.

In order to understand why that is, it might help to understand a little about the main differences between the Theravada and Mahayana approaches to the Dharma. Theravada is the oldest extant Buddhist school and is doctrinally the closest to what Gotama Buddha actually taught in his lifetime. The goal of Theravada practice is to seek the most direct route to Enlightenment in order to escape the suffering inherent in the rounds of birth, or *samsara*. Theravada Buddhists seek to apply the Dharma as taught by the Buddha to their lives. One who is fully enlightened by following the teachings of a Buddha is called an *arahant*. Like Buddhas, *arahants* attain Nirvana when they die but are unable to teach the Dharma to others with the level of effectiveness that Buddhas can; they have not cultivated certain perfections of character over the rounds of rebirth to the extent that Buddhas have. In short, a Theravadin seeks their own Enlightenment as an *arahant* as quickly as possible but not to become a Buddha, as this takes far more lifetimes to achieve.

The main difference between a Buddha and an *arahant* is that a Buddha is one who *discovers* the Dharma in an age when nobody knows of it, as Gotama Buddha did around 530 BCE,

---

[74] There are, of course, branches of Christianity that do not fall into one of these categories, such as the Coptic, Nestorian, and Armenian churches, but these collectively make up only a small percentage of the worldwide Christian population.

rather than practicing the Dharma as taught by a Buddha who has already discovered it. Because of the sheer amount of time (and births) it takes to become a Buddha, the path to becoming one is necessarily more difficult than that of an *arahant*. *Bodhisattvas*, or beings who seek to become Buddhas, intentionally delay their own Enlightenment in order to walk this higher path. The main benefit of the bodhisattva path is not for the person walking it, but rather for others. Buddhas have a much stronger ability to help others reach Enlightenment than *arahants* do, and so bodhisattvas essentially refuse Nirvana until they can most effectively bring others along with them.

In other words, the main difference between Theravada and Mahayana Buddhists is the goal of practice. Theravadins seek to become *arahants*, while Mahayana practitioners mostly try to become bodhisattvas and, ultimately, Buddhas. I chose to practice Theravada Buddhism because I seek the quickest route to Enlightenment, and I recognize that waiting for others is subject to impermanence; for example, how can I be sure that others will want to progress at the same pace I do? To what extent am I willing to alter my own goals for the sake of others? However, I realize that many others do not feel this way. Many Buddhists prefer to make sure others can achieve Nirvana with them and that is one reason why the Mahayana school, including its Vajrayana offshoot, has more adherents than the Theravada both in Asia and the West.[75]

Accordingly, I think it would be helpful to discuss a story of one of the Æsir geared toward those who feel attracted to Mahayana practice. The story concerns the god Tyr and in many ways mirrors some of the stories about Odin. Ásatrúar consider Tyr to be the "boldest and most courageous"[76] of the gods and venerate him for many reasons, but he is best known for ridding the world of the scourge of Fenrir. Fenrir is a wolf—the son of Loki,

[75] There are also other reasons. Theravada Buddhists mostly live in Myanmar, Thailand, Laos, Cambodia, and Sri Lanka, while Buddhists in Japan, Korea, Vietnam, and China generally practice the Mahayana path. The sheer size of China's population makes Mahayana the largest school in Asia. Tibetans mostly practice Vajrayana, which, owing to the Dalai Lama and other Tibetan teachers finding refuge abroad after the Chinese occupation of their country, has become the most popular school of Buddhism in the West.

[76] Snorri Sturluson, *The Prose Edda*, trans. Jesse L. Byock (London: Penguin, 2005), 36.

god of mischief, and Angrboða, a female Jötunn, or giant—prophesied to bring great harm and misfortune to the Æsir.

Attempting to foil these prophecies, the Æsir twice attempted to bind Fenrir in iron chains, which the wolf took as challenges and easily escaped both times. Exasperated, some of the gods visited dwarves who made "a fetter . . . smooth and soft as a silk ribbon, yet . . .reliable and strong,"[77] which its makers called Gleipnir. The gods again challenged Fenrir to let them bind him, but Fenrir was a little suspicious this time. He thought there must have been some kind of trickery in the crafting of Gleipnir because it looked so much less imposing than the iron binds he had already broken. Fenrir told the Æsir that he would let them bind him only if one of the gods would place their hand in his mouth as insurance that they were not trying to fool him.

The Æsir realized that the jig was up; Fenrir had figured them out. Nobody knew what to do until Tyr "raised his right hand and laid it in the wolf's mouth." Fenrir quickly realized that Gleipnir was unbreakable and promptly bit off Tyr's hand. The gods chained Fenrir under the earth, and there he will remain until Ragnarök, when he will kill Odin (and thus fulfill the prophecy).

Like Odin, Tyr was willing to sacrifice a part of his physical body in order to become something *more*. One could take this as evidence that he เข้าใจ the body's impermanent, suffering nature. Knowing that Ragnarök is inevitable, knowing that no creature can keep its body together indefinitely anyway, and being unattached to any view that *my life will be better with my hand* or that *my hand is indeed mine,*[78] which would be a wrong view based on the illusion of permanence, made Tyr able to willingly sacrifice his appendage for the good of the Æsir and for the world at large. The fact that he was willing to make this sacrifice not for knowledge and wisdom, as Odin did, nor for any personal benefit as such, but rather largely on behalf of others demonstrates the perfection of character of a bodhisattva on the path to Buddhahood.

---

[77] Sturluson, 41

[78] For more, see the Buddha's sermon on the characteristic of nonself in the *Khandasaṃutta* of the *Saṃyutta Nikāya* (SN 22.59), found in Bhikkhu Bodhi, trans., *The Connected Discourses of the Buddha: A Translation of the Saṃyutta Nikāya* (Boston: Wisdom Publications, 2000), 901–3.

To walk the path of a bodhisattva, one must be willing to put one's own goals behind that of the collective. I honor and respect those who make that choice; after all, without Buddhas, the Dharma remains obscured and difficult to see. It is necessary for someone to choose that path. However, it is also important to know oneself. I wouldn't be able to do that, and that is why I chose to practice the Theravada school of Buddhism. However, I hope that this story about Tyr's sacrifice inspires those who feel drawn to the Mahayana path.

Chapter 11: Conclusion: Time to Leave the Cave

One of the ancient Athenian philosopher Plato's most well known ideas is his allegory of the cave. It appears in Book VII of his seminal work *The Republic*. The allegory describes a hypothetical scenario in which humans spend their entire lives within a cave, only able to see reflections of sunlight and shadows of objects that pass in front of its entrance. These unfortunate perma-spelunkers are unable to see the sun itself, nor the actual objects that create the shadows. They therefore "hold that the truth is nothing other than the shadows of artificial things."[79] Plato posits that this is essentially the position in which humanity finds itself— blinded by the limitations of our world and our perceptions of it without the inclination to seek the truth beyond these asymptotes—though all one really needs to do in order to "see the light" is stand up and walk outside.

Plato then describes what might happen if a man in his cave were indeed to stand up, go out in the sun, and look around. He suggests that at first, this man would be frightened, that his eyes would "hurt and he would flee, turning away to those things that he is able to make out and hold them to be really clearer" than what he sees outside the cave. However, after "becoming accustomed" to the new circumstance, he would see the source and "cause of all those things he and his companions had been seeing.:"[80] After doing so, "any honors, praises, and prizes" given by the cave dwellers would become meaningless to him, and he would "undergo anything whatsoever rather than to opine those things and live that way."

Seeing and accepting the truth of this world makes one unfit to live in it. (Christ echoes this in the Gospel of Thomas, writing, "Whosoever has come to know the world has discovered a carcass, and of that person the world is not worthy."[81]) Plato believed that we are all living in this shadow world, seeing only part of the truth and turning it into the entire truth in our minds. Even some of us who see brief glimpses of the truth find it

---

[79] Plato, *The Republic*, trans. Allan Bloom (New York: Basic, 1968), 194.
[80] Plato, 195.
[81] Martin Meyer, trans., *The Gospel of Thomas* (San Francisco: Harper, 1992), 45.

uncomfortable and yearn to return to a world that makes sense according to our cherished perceptions. St. Augustine wrote of this, "I had prayed to you for chastity and said 'Lord, make me pure, but not yet!' For I was afraid that you would answer my prayer at once and cure me too soon of the disease of lust, which I wanted satisfied, not quelled."[82]

This allegory of the cave encapsulates the idea of Enlightenment nearly perfectly. Each of us has *micchā diṭṭhi*, or wrong views, in our minds and hearts. They are based on some permanent assumption like "what I see before my eyes represents the full extent of reality." One who เข้าใจ impermanence can see beyond these wrong views, that there are more possibilities in every situation than a single person can imagine, and that each of us must make the effort to overcome our tendency to see things in only one way. If we can do so, the importance of honors and accolades of this world will fade, and we can stop struggling so hard to obtain them.

Plato is not the only Greek philosopher who has grappled with this dharmic idea; his student Aristotle, the most preeminent of premodern Western philosophers, tackled this problem in his *Nicomachean Ethics*. In Book Two of this important work, Aristotle introduces the Doctrine of the Mean, which essentially suggests that the best way to live is halfway between extremes of personality. He lists personality traits and divides them into thirds: excess, deficiency, and mean. One should aim at the mean at all times.

For example, regarding self-expression, the three possibilities are boastfulness (excess), understatement (deficiency), and truthfulness (mean). Aristotle divides shame into shyness, shamelessness, and modesty; and honor into vanity, pusillanimity, and magnanimity[83]. When one reads Aristotle's words, it is immediately clear that the Middle Paths he selects are ideal because they shy away from a sense of permanence.

Consider self-expression. The excess and the mean are both instinctive reactions. Boastful and understated people have

---

[82] Augustine of Hippo, *Confessions*, trans. R. S. Pine-Coffin (London: Penguin, 1961), 169.
[83] Aristotle, *Ethics,* trans. J.A.K. Thompson. (London: Penguin, 1955), 104.

an idea that their accomplishments should *always* be met with a certain reaction, either under- or overstated. Boastful people have the wrong view that their accomplishments are always worth trumpeting, and understated people believe that they aren't worthwhile. Boastfulness is a disagreeable trait to most people, and understatement can also be annoying in its way over time. *Truthfulness* is the mean and the ideal because it is based on the principle of impermanence. Truthful people are honest about their accomplishments, neither bragging about them nor playing them down. They simply state fact, without attaching anything to it.

This is what the Buddha meant by the Middle Path. Buddhists strive to achieve this Middle Path, or put another way, the Aristotelian Mean, and speak honestly and simply not only with others but more importantly, with themselves. Indulging in interpretation of fact is bound to push the limits of human perception and therefore create impressions based on imagination. Such imaginations have shaky foundations and will sooner or later be exposed as such by circumstance, causing a large amount of suffering. Having no *need* for things to be one way or the other but accepting change within one's heart, not trying to control the uncontrollable, is a goal in line with Aristotle's prescription and a path to inner peace.

The idea that an excess or a deficiency leads to bad consequences exists in Christianity as well. Dante structures the entire *Inferno* along these lines. The upper reaches of Hell are populated with those who loved earthly things too much (such as the lustful and gluttonous). As one descends, one finds the violent and fraudulent—those whose sins resulted from a lack of love. Dante inverts this structure in *Purgatorio*. The lower levels of Purgatory proper are populated by the proud, envious, and wrathful who are guilty of improper love. The slothful suffered from a deficiency of love, and the avaricious, gluttonous, and lustful are guilty of an excess of love (for earthly things). This is a powerful metaphor because it suggests that even something that nearly every person regards as "good," namely love, can lead to grave consequences if pursued in an imbalanced way.

That is ultimately the lesson of this book. The Buddha taught that all suffering comes from within. The world cannot make you suffer; only you can do that. If this is not already true about you, imagine for a moment that you are very short. Perhaps others tease you from time to time about your height. Can you control what others do? You may plead with them, reason with them, or appeal to their sense of kindness, and perhaps they will relent. And yet, perhaps they will not! It is not within your power to make others, and by extension the world, conform to your wishes and expectations. The only way to stop suffering if others tease you about your height is to accept in your heart that you are shorter than most other people - to เข้าใจ the truth. Once you accept that, it will not hurt anymore if someone teases you about your height. It will be as if they are calling the sky blue. What power does a bully have if you say, "Yeah, I'm short. So what?" Inner acceptance of the truth, เข้าใจ, quells the fire in the heart and makes the machinations of the world outside essentially irrelevant.

Accordingly, the Buddha taught that the path to peace and freedom lies within you. Christ echoes this sentiment when he says, "The kingdom is inside you and it is outside you. When you know yourselves, then you will be known . . . but if you do not know yourselves, then you will dwell in poverty."[84]. It is up to each and every one of us to find our wrong, permanent views when emotions arise within us, as Odin, Thor, and Christ himself did, and as circumstance forced the prodigal son's brother and the vineyard workers to do. We must admit the truth in our hearts *of ourselves to ourselves* and bend our hearts toward accepting what is rather than pining for what we may prefer. As Queen Ubbari and Dante's souls on the banks of the Acheron discovered, we may be blind to the fact that what we want may be horrifying!

It's rare that popular music can convey dharmic truth, but I've always loved the song "Overstand" by Dead Prez. The outro summarizes the point I'm trying to make very well:

"Change is necessary for evolution
The universe contains incredible diversity
And you cannot experience it all within the confines of one comfortable lifestyle
Look ahead to what you will think of your life at its end

---

[84] *The Gospel of Thomas*, 23.

You will probably not want to look back and say it was cozy and dull
Thus, react positively to what seems to be disaster
Remember that what seems now to be disaster may be an important step toward evolution
And may even be identifiable as such at some point in the future
Every great loss takes you out of a rut and starts life anew
Be grateful for the time you had and your former happy state
And look forward eagerly to the new phase."[85]

I hope that the ideas and stories in this book originating from Western religion, as well as my own experiences, have given you a template upon which you can begin to contemplate your own experiences and *micchā diṭṭhi*. Armed with this knowledge, I hope you can เข้าใจ Dharma, or universal truth, as you seek to เข้าใจ yourself and your heart. It is my wish that you begin to see impermanence in all things and realize that your suffering begins from your own limited perspective. Sometimes, disasters are fertilizer for great things to come.

Let us together stand up and walk out of the cave! Like St. Augustine, let's let go of our old vices and attachments and become the people we are meant to become. Once we do so, what seems so important within the cave will no longer entice us. There is nothing to fear except what is within us, but what seems scary and difficult now will no longer be important when we blossom and bloom together, showing the world the brilliance of the colors encased inside of our fears. Remember *always* that beautiful trees like Yggdrasil and lotus flowers alike grow out of dirt.

---

[85] Dead Prez, "Overstand," track 13 on *Information Age* Deluxe Edition, Krian Music Group, 2012, vinyl.

Bibliography

Works Cited

Alighieri, Dante. *The Divine Comedy.* Translated by John Ciardi. New York: New American Library, 2003.

Aristotle. *Ethics.* Translated by J.A.K. Thompson. London: Penguin, 1955.

Augustine of Hippo. *Confessions.* Translated by R. S. Pine-Coffin. London: Penguin, 1961.

Bodhi, Bhikkhu, trans. *The Connected Discourses of the Buddha: A Translation of the Saṃyutta Nikāya.* Boston: Wisdom Publications, 2000.

Bodhi, Bhikkhu, and Bhikkhu Nanamoli, trans. *The Middle Length Discourses of the Buddha: A Translation of the Majjhima Nikāya.* Boston: Wisdom Publications, 2005.

Confucius. *The Analects.* Translated by Raymond Dawson. Oxford: Oxford University Press, 1993.

Dead Prez. *Information Age* Deluxe Edition. Krian Music Group, 2012, vinyl.

Durant, Will. *Our Oriental Heritage.* New York: Fine Communications, 1997.

Holy Bible: Authorized King James Version. New York: Harper, 1930.

Larrington, Carolyne, trans. *The Poetic Edda.* Oxford: Oxford University Press, 1996.

Meyer, Martin, trans. *The Gospel of Thomas.* San Francisco: Harper, 1992.

Newton, Isaac. *Newton's Principia: The Mathematical Principles of Natural Philosophy.* Translated by Andrew Motte. New York: Daniel Adee, 1846.

Plato. *The Republic.* Translated by Allan Bloom. New York: Basic, 1968.

Roebuck, Valerie J., trans. *The Dhammapada.* London: Penguin, 2010.

Sandars, N. K., trans. *The Epic of Gilgamesh.* London: Penguin, 1960.

Sturluson, Snorri. *The Prose Edda*. Translated by Jesse L. Byock. London: Penguin, 2005.

Walshe, Maurice, trans. *The Long Discourses of the Buddha: A Translation of the Dīgha Nikāya*. Boston: Wisdom Publications, 1987.

Works Consulted

Acariya Thoon Khippapanno Bhikkhu. *Going Against the Stream*. Bangkok: P. Samphan Panhanich, 2003.

Anandapanyo Bhikkhu. *Right Start, Right Finish: Buddhism*. San Francisco: San Fran Dhammaram, 2001.

The Bhagavad Gita. Translated by Eknath Easwaran. Tomales, CA: Nilgiri, 2007.

Homer. *The Iliad*. Translated by Robert Fagles. London: Penguin, 1978.

Kant, Immanuel. *Kritik der reinen Vernunft*. Köln: Anaconda Verlag, 2013.

The Ramayana. Translated by R. K. Narayan. London: Penguin, 1972.

Rousseau, Jean-Jacques. *The Social Contract*. Translated by Maurice Cranston. London: Penguin, 1968.

Acknowledgements

First and foremost, I'd like to thank my Dharma teachers at Wat San Fran Dhammaram in San Francisco: Mae Yo, Mae Neecha, Phra Anandapanyo, and Phra Nuttapanyo, as well as the lay community there. Their teaching and guidance means the world to me, and I continue to feel immense gratitude to the group for taking in a Western outsider and teaching me the Dharma. Sadhu to the late Phra Ajan Deng of Wat Pa Ban Koh in Udon Thani, Thailand, who allowed me to experience the presence of an arahant.

I also owe a debt of gratitude to the late Reverend Carlton Payne, who was the pastor at St. Matthew's Lutheran Church in Lake Zurich, Illinois when I was a teenager. His guidance, kindness, patience, and mentorship set me on my spiritual path all those years ago, though I didn't realize it until much later.

Thanks to my parents, my brother Alexander, and Sophie Frank, all of whose level-headed advice continues to provide me with perspective on a daily basis. I also appreciate all of my students, for they are in many ways my most important teachers.

Finally, sadhu to Gregor Everitt, the editor of this text. I couldn't have done it without you.

Your Notes

Made in the USA
Middletown, DE
24 February 2023

25318860R00046